American Material Culture and the Texas Experience

The David B. Warren Symposium

Volume 2

American Material Culture and the Texas Experience

The David B. Warren Symposium

Volume 2

Bayou Bend Collection and Gardens
The Museum of Fine Arts, Houston

This publication is based on papers delivered at the second David B. Warren Symposium, "American Material Culture and the Texas Experience," presented by Bayou Bend Collection and Gardens at the Museum of Fine Arts, Houston, on October 30–31, 2009.

If you would like to support the Endowment Fund for the biennial David B. Warren Symposium, please send your contribution to Bayou Bend Collection and Gardens, P. O. Box 6826, Houston, Texas 77265-6826.

Edited by Christine Waller Manca
Book design by Phenon Finley-Smiley
Printing by Masterpiece Litho, Inc.

Printed in the United States of America

Library of Congress Cataloging-in-Publication Data

David B. Warren Symposium.
    American material culture and the Texas experience : the David B. Warren Symposium.
        p. cm.
    ISBN 978-0-89090-173-1 (pbk. : alk. paper)
    1. Decorative arts--United States--Congresses. I. Bayou Bend Collection. II. Museum of Fine Arts, Houston. III. Title.
    NK805.D35 2009
    745.0973--dc22
                            2009000711

*Front cover: Thomas Flintoff. **Portrait of the Jones Children of Galveston.** c. 1852. Oil on canvas. The Bayou Bend Collection, gift of Miss Ima Hogg (B.59.132).*

Back cover: Bayou Bend, north facade.

*Frontispiece: Thomas Flintoff. **Catholic Church, Houston, Texas.** 1852. Watercolor. The Bayou Bend Collection, gift of Cynthia Petrello in honor of Carena Petrello at "One Great Night in November, 2007 (B.2007.9).*

The 2009 David B. Warren Symposium was made possible in part by a grant from Humanities Texas, the state affiliate of the National Endowment for the Humanities; the Texas Historical Foundation; and CASETA (Center for the Advancement and Study of Early Texas Art).

The David B. Warren Symposium receives permanent income from endowment funds provided by Isabel B. and Wallace S. Wilson, Mr. and Mrs. Mark Abendshein, the Audrey Jones Beck Estate, The Brown Foundation, Inc., Betsy D. and Hugh Ghormley, Lora Jean Kilroy, and Mr. and Mrs. Robert P. Ross, Jr.

Additional endowment gifts were received from the George and Anne Butler Foundation, Lee and Joe Jamail, the Kennedy Trust, the John P. McGovern Foundation, the Stedman West Foundation, Mr. and Mrs. Charles W. Tate, Mr. Fayez Sarofim, Mr. and Mrs. A. Clark Johnson, Dr. and Mrs. F. R. Lummis, Jr., and the Payne Foundation.

Contents

Directors' Foreword

"Without Ima Hogg, there would be virtually no early American material culture in Texas today. Not surprisingly, the greatest concentration of examples…in the state is here in Houston. Nearly all the other important collecting of Americana in Houston was influenced, in one way or another, by Ima Hogg's collecting and by her gift of her collection to the public." — David B. Warren, 2007

Bayou Bend Collection and Gardens is uniquely suited to present a biennial symposium on pre-1900 American material culture from a Texas perspective. The collection's founder Ima Hogg (1882–1975) was a native Texan who focused much of her life and philanthropy on preserving and educating people about the early heritage of America (1620–1876) and of Texas (the 1800s). In addition to featuring one of the world's finest collections of early American decorative arts and painting, Bayou Bend displays major examples of nineteenth-century Texas furniture, silver, ceramics, and painting.

In 1957, Miss Hogg formally announced her intention to give the Bayou Bend estate and her collection to the Museum of Fine Arts, Houston. She worked for ten years to oversee the transition of the 1920s mansion from private residence to public museum. At the opening of Bayou Bend in 1966, she said: "Texas, an empire in itself, geographically and historically, sometimes seems to be regarded as remote or alien to the rest of our nation. I hope in a modest way that Bayou Bend may serve as a bridge to bring us closer to the heart of an American heritage which unites us." This statement has become an iconic definition of Bayou Bend's educational mission and an excellent framework for a scholarly series that aims to place the early material culture of Texas, as well as the South and Southwest, within a national and international context.

It was fitting to name the symposium series for David B. Warren, Bayou Bend's founding director emeritus, since it was he whom Ima Hogg hired in 1965 to guide Bayou Bend—which he subsequently did with great dedication and scholarship over a distinguished thirty-eight-year tenure. Appropriately the keynote speaker at the 2007 inaugural symposium, David discussed Ima Hogg's vision for Bayou Bend and her love for her national and state heritage, setting the stage for all future symposia.

Bayou Bend, north facade

Following are the proceedings of the second David B. Warren Symposium, organized by Bayou Bend and museum staff and held at the Museum of Fine Arts, Houston, on October 30–31, 2009. The papers, presented by five talented and respected scholars from across the country, are organized around the year's sub-theme: art and architecture before 1900 in Texas, the South, and the Southwest.

Given that when first made, the objects in the Bayou Bend Collection were primarily intended for display or use in a domestic setting, the publication opens with a fascinating discussion on the "roots of home" by architect and historian Russell Versaci. The essay journeys across the American South, examining the wide range of architectural styles that developed there during the seventeenth, eighteenth, and nineteenth centuries. Building on Versaci's introduction of the Germanic tradition behind the Texas rock house style, Kenneth Hafertepe delves into a study of these mid-nineteenth-century houses that were built by German immigrants to central Texas—examining how the living spaces were arranged, and what materials and methods were used in their construction.

These architectural discussions are joined by three art historical essays which demonstrate that an equally broad range of influences and traditions can be identified in the art produced in Texas, the South, and the Southwest prior to 1900. Sam Ratcliffe expertly addresses the European Romantic roots of Texas painting—English, Irish, and French to some extent, but primarily German. Maurie D. McInnis uses the 1939 film *Gone with the Wind* to present a thought-provoking analysis of the English-based landscape tradition in the South—picturesque, idealized, and in the post-Civil-War era, often imbued with a sense of loss. Michael R. Grauer's concluding paper on early paintings of the American Southwest suggests that the untouched, dramatic beauty of the western lands led artists beyond their American and European influences in their attempt to capture God's glory spread out before them.

By publishing the proceedings of each symposium, the museum is helping to build a much-needed critical literature on the material culture of Texas, the lower South, and the Southwest, placing it within the broader field of American material culture. The publications, as well as the symposia themselves, are possible thank to the guidance, assistance, and support of many individuals and organizations. Our special thanks to the trustees of the Museum of Fine Arts, Houston, and the members of the

Bayou Bend Committee, for supporting the symposium concept and the creation of a symposium endowment fund. A list of the endowment's lead donors may be found at the front of this publication, but we wish to recognize here, as well, Isabel B. and Wallace S. Wilson, Mr. and Mrs. Mark Abendshein, the Audrey Jones Beck Estate, The Brown Foundation, Inc., Betsy D. Ghormley, Lora Jean (Jeanie) Kilroy, and Mr. and Mrs. Robert P. Ross, Jr. There is an ongoing effort to increase the endowment to ensure the future growth and success of the symposium initiative.

The 2009 symposium would not have been possible without additional generous support from Humanities Texas, the state affiliate of the National Endowment for the Humanities; the Texas Historical Foundation; and CASETA (Center for the Advancement and Study of Early Texas Art). Special thanks as well to Bayou Bend's dear friend and supporter Mrs. Frederick R. Lummis for hosting the Speaker's Dinner.

As this volume goes to print, we remember the legacy of Peter C. Marzio, director of the Museum of Fine Arts, Houston, from 1982 to 2010. He wanted Bayou Bend to play a greater regional and national role in encouraging research in early American material culture, and he believed that Bayou Bend's Kitty King Powell Library and Study Center, located in the new Lora Jean Kilroy Visitor and Education Center, would help further that goal. He viewed the David B. Warren Symposium on American Material Culture and the Texas Experience as an excellent example of the positive impact the museum could have on advancing scholarship in the varied fields of research encompassed by Bayou Bend Collection and Gardens.

Gwendolyn H. Goffe
Interim Director
The Museum of Fine Arts, Houston

Bonnie A. Campbell
Director
Bayou Bend Collection and Gardens

Roots of Home:
An Architectural Tourist in the South

Russell Versaci

"If architecture is the physical evidence of history, certainly history makes a tremendous impact on architecture. . . . Thus if you will understand architecture, you must also know history." —Albert Manucy, *The Houses of St. Augustine* (1962)

I am an architect and a historian. I love all things old, and I love to seek out their stories. History is my compass, my field guide, my book of rules, and my inspiration for designing new houses for people today. Architecture is my lens for viewing history.

Architecture opens a unique window on the origins, history, society, and culture of a place and the character and aspirations of its inhabitants. By studying buildings, I learn how people settled and cultivated places, how places have changed over time, and what promises they hold for the future.

Figs. 1–4. Examples of early colonial American houses (clockwise from top left): Jethro Coffin House, Nantucket, Massachusetts, 1686; Don Raimundo Arrivas House, Saint Augustine, Florida, c. 1650–1700; Joiner Farmhouse, Suffolk County, Virginia; and Jonathan Hager House, Hagerstown, Maryland, 1739.

I am also an architectural tourist. When I travel, I like to wander the back roads of America seeking old houses that are worn and weathered by time. I rummage through the attic of architecture in search of precedents in order to design new houses in classic American styles. Each of the houses I design is an adventure, and each adventure begins with history.

In America, we have four centuries of building traditions to explore. From coast to coast, there are classic regional styles born from a mix of cultural heritage, climate, geography, and natural resources that are unique to their locales (figs. 1–4). These historical forces have shaped the traditions of America's favorite places. I call them the "roots of home."

What are the roots of the architecture of the South? We know its hallmarks— plantation houses and raised cottages, shotguns and crackers, casitas and dogtrots, with catslide roofs and camelbacks, piazzas and porticoes, lanterns and blinds, magnolias and live oaks—but few of us know where they came from. To find the roots of Southern home styles, we need to go back in time to the beginnings of American history, back to Old World Europe.

Old World Origins

"We Americans have yet to really learn our own antecedents . . . We tacitly abandon ourselves to the notion that our United States have been fashioned from the British Islands only . . . which is a very great mistake."
    —Walt Whitman, *The Spanish Element in Our Nationality,* 1883

When Christopher Columbus set sail in 1492 on his epic voyage for Ferdinand and Isabella of Spain, he was looking for a way west to expand trade with Cathay (China) and the Spice Islands of the Indies. Charting a new westerly course, he had no idea that he was sailing toward the dawn of a new age. When he stumbled upon the islands of the Caribbean, he thought he had reached the Indies and called the native people Indios, or Indians. In time it became quite clear that this was not the Indies at all, but an unknown new land on which he had planted the flag of Spain.

When news of Spain's discovery reached Europe, it set off a firestorm of envy among the monarchs of Portugal, France, Denmark, England, and the republic of the Netherlands, all of whom were vying for empires and trade around the globe. Colonization became an entrepreneurial enterprise for all of the great powers. Yet for nearly a century the Spanish plundered the riches of the Caribbean while

*Fig. 5. Map illustrating the "ten colonial cradles
of home." Russell Versaci Architecture.*

fending off European competitors who wanted to take a piece of their discovery.

As a result of Spain's domination of the southern New World, other Old
World entrepreneurs were forced to look further north, to a continent the
Spaniards had decided held little of value—no gold, no silver, no precious stones—
North America. The French, English, and Dutch made the best of it, coming to
trade with the Indians, cultivate plantations, seek religious asylum, and Christianize
the natives. They were patricians and paupers, merchants and farmers, servants and
slaves, missionaries and thieves. The places where this mixed diaspora settled became
cradles of colonial home building that were as diverse as their settlements were
unique (fig. 5).

While the Spanish settled missions in the Florida peninsula and southwest
borderlands, the French scattered roots in the St. Lawrence Valley, Great Lakes,
Mississippi Valley, and Gulf Coast. The Dutch set up trading posts and boweries
in the Hudson Valley, and the English built plantations around Chesapeake Bay and

*Figs. 6–7. Examples of Old World building traditions, reconstructed at the Museum of Frontier Culture in Staunton, Virginia (top to bottom): an eighteenth-century Irish fieldstone farmhouse from County Tyrone, Ulster; and a seventeenth-century German half-timber **Fachwerk** farmhouse.*

the Carolina tidewater, as well as religious utopias in New England. These first settlements became the colonial cradles of home where the American nation was born.

Birth of a Nation

America's architectural journey began with Old World styles that washed ashore in the baggage of early European colonists (figs. 6–7). They built homes that blended memory and experience in equal measure, adapting the European building traditions they knew to the practical requirements of New World climates, geography, and natural resources. Some things worked well, while others had to change. Over time regional traditions began to take root that were pragmatic as well as innovative—and distinctly American in flavor.

They were also portable. As succeeding generations moved out to the frontier, pioneers brought with them what they had learned in the original colonies. Styles of homebuilding migrated and were transplanted into fresh soil, retaining aspects of their earlier character while being reshaped to fit new places. Over centuries of slow change, these early colonial roots evolved into classic American house styles.

Today we know these styles by their regional identities—New England colonial, Pennsylvania Dutch, Virginia Tidewater, Louisiana Creole, Southwest adobe, California Mission. Each style represents the cumulative history of generations of builders adapting to our new land. But to many of us, their early stories are virtually unknown. Where did these classic house forms come from? How did they evolve into the historic homes we know and love today? What can we learn from them to design new houses inspired by history?

In the South, the colonial cradles began in the Chesapeake Tidewater, the Carolina Low Country, the Florida Peninsula, the Gulf Coast, the Mississippi Valley, and of course, in Texas. The tale of Captain John Smith and his band of English adventurers who settled Jamestown in 1607 has often been told and is canonized in American folklore. Therefore, we will begin with the intriguing story of that most southern of cities—Charleston, South Carolina.

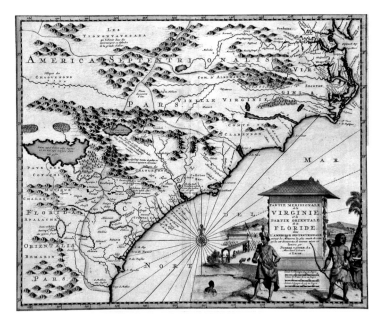

Fig. 8. Eighteenth-century map of the Carolina Low Country. Pieter van der Aa.
Partie Meridionale de la Virginie*. 1729.*

Fig. 9. Charleston Single House, East Bay and Reid Street, Charleston, South Carolina.

Charleston Single House

"All Artificers, as Carpenters, Wheelwrights, Joyners, Coopers, Bricklayers, Smiths, or diligent Husbandmen and Labourers, that are willing to advance their fortunes, may take notice that . . . they have made a Town, called Charles-Town, where there is plenty of as rich ground as any in the world."

—Robert Horne, *A Brief Description of the Province of Carolina* (1666)

Beginning in the 1660s, English colonists from the West Indies migrated to the Carolina Low Country, lured there by a group of eight English lords proprietors who had received a land grant from King Charles II (fig. 8). Among them were Sir John Colleton and a band of English planters from Barbados who departed the island to seek their fortunes in Carolina's fertile soils. For nearly fifty years, they had practiced building in the tropical Caribbean, from which they imported the raised plantation with covered verandas and shallow roofs to the humid, subtropical Carolinas. Their house forms became the townhouses of Charleston and the plantation houses of the tidewater coast.

Founded in 1670, Charleston was the principal port and market town for the Carolina colony. Merchant ships departed Charleston's docks daily, bringing crops of rice and indigo across the sea to England. Enriched by trade, the new plantation aristocracy created a metropolis filled with Georgian townhouses and all the trappings of tasteful English life.

In the opening years of the eighteenth century, a house style was born that became a signature of the city—the Charleston single house (fig. 9). The single house is named for a floor plan that is only a single room deep to promote cross-ventilation. Tall and slender, often three stories in height, the single house is offset to one side of its lot, with a narrow facade that faces the street and a long, formal front that faces a private side yard.

In early Charleston, the side yard between adjacent houses was a workplace—a long, narrow outdoor space containing a carriage way, a vegetable garden, and even a few cows and chickens. In later years, this space was transformed into an elegant formal garden, providing gracious outdoor living space. Behind the house were a separate office and kitchen, a "necessary," and often a carriage house, with servants' quarters above the outbuildings.

The crown jewel of the single house is its two-story piazza, a double porch that runs down the length of the long side, sheltering doors and windows from the sun and providing relief from the hot, humid climate. Typically, piazzas are stacked one

Fig. 10. Miles Brewton House, Charleston, South Carolina, c. 1765–69.

above the other so that all rooms have access to a porch. Before air-conditioning, the piazza served as an outdoor living room and cool sleeping area with shutter panels between its columns for privacy.

Charleston's most bountiful years began in the 1760s after the French and Indian War, when the streets filled with Georgian single houses built in clapboard, brick, and stucco. By the time the Revolutionary War began in 1775, wealthy traders like Miles Brewton and William Gibbes had brought another traditional style to Charleston from Georgian London—the double house (fig. 10).

In fact, the double house is not two single houses joined together, but a center-hall Georgian colonial built on a wide building lot. The Brewton and Gibbes houses have symmetrical facades facing the street and ornamental porticoes framing the front door. The lineage of the double house comes from the work of English architects James Gibbs, Robert Adam, William Chambers, and others whose fashionable classical townhouses filled mid-eighteenth-century London.

Fig. 11. Ford Plantation House, Donald Rattner, architect.

The classic homes of Charleston have inspired a contemporary revival of a house form still well suited to today's Low Country. Architect Donald Rattner has mastered the style in his design for a new single house at the Ford Plantation in coastal Georgia (fig. 11). On one of the neighborhood's deep, narrow lots, the architect has created a new home adorned with elegant piazzas in a spirited reinvention of the hallmark style of Charleston architecture.

Like the trademark houses of Charleston, the recent house sits right next to the sidewalk. It stands three stories tall above a ground floor of handmade bricks, raised up to protect the house from damp soils, insects, and flooding. The upper floors are cream-colored stucco, like Charleston's early stucco-covered houses painted in pastel shades of yellow, pink, green, and blue. The long side of the house carries a double piazza that catches sea breezes rolling across Georgia's coastal salt marshes. This new Charleston single house is a fitting adaptation to the sultry climate of the Low Country.

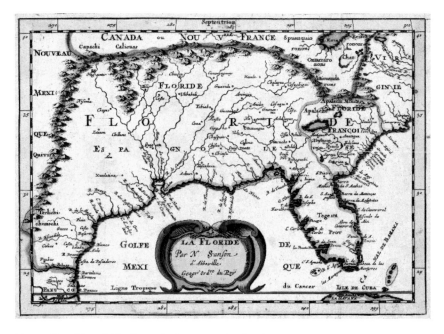

Fig. 12. Map of Spanish Florida. Nicolas Sanson. *La Floride*. 1657.
Geography and Map Division, Library of Congress, Washington, D.C.

St. Augustine Style

"The houses [of St. Augustine] are built quite after the Spanish fashion, with flat roofs and few windows. . . . Here and there the English have houses with more windows, especially on the street side. . . . Almost every house has its little garden, of which splendid lemon and orange trees are not the least ornaments."

—William Bartram, *Travels* (1791)

The houses of old St. Augustine, Florida, share a legacy of more than four centuries of living by Spanish, English, and American owners. The oldest permanent city in America, the port town of St. Augustine was founded by Spaniards in 1565 as a natural harbor to protect Spain's treasure fleet as it sailed through the Straits of Florida toward Seville.

The Spanish settled Florida a half-century before the English set foot in Jamestown, coming to North America by way of the Spanish West Indies (fig. 12). Christened San Agustin de la Florida, St. Augustine was founded by Pedro

Menendez de Aviles, a Spanish naval commander who brought to La Florida a mix of sailors, soldiers, and settlers from Cuba, Hispaniola, and Spain. He laid out the town as a grid of streets and building lots formally arranged around a central plaza as dictated by the Spanish Laws of the Indies.

In the West Indies, the Spanish had learned how to adapt their Old World building skills to the New World by building in local woods, stucco, and stone. On Anastasia Island near St. Augustine, they found ledges of coral shellstone, called coquina, easily cut into building blocks. They shaped coquina into casas of simple, sturdy block walls that were one story tall, covered with flat roofs of clay supported by wooden beams, much like the adobe casas of the Southwest. The plain walls were plastered with stucco and painted with lime-wash for weatherproofing.

The Spaniards built masonry houses in St. Augustine for 200 years, until the English took over in 1763. From then on, St. Augustine became a town of layered history. Rather than tearing down the old Spanish casas, the English improvised on top of them with their own traditions. They added second stories of wood beneath sloped roofs and covered the new walls with clapboard siding, a building technique they had used on plantation houses in the British West Indies.

The English grafted another centuries-old West Indies tradition onto the old Spanish houses—the suspended balcony (fig. 13). St. Augustine's balconies are cantilevered out over the street on second-floor beams that run through the walls,

Fig. 13. Ximénez-Fatio House, St. Augustine, Florida, 1798.

Fig. 14. Fernández-Llambias House, St. Augustine, Florida, c. 1750.

Fig. 15. González-Alvarez House, St. Augustine, Florida, c. 1715–75.

creating private sitting porches that have no support posts below. These street balconies have become the hallmark of the St. Augustine style.

Today in St. Augustine's historic district, restored houses record the legacy of Spanish, English, and American layers. While there are no wooden houses that survive from the earliest period, many of the Spanish casas made of coquina stone are still with us, often beneath a history of additions that obscure the way they once looked.

Among dozens of well-preserved houses, the Fernandez-Llambias House (fig. 14) is the most memorable portrait of a true St. Augustine colonial home. Built during the second Spanish period of 1702–63, the earliest part of the house is a single-story casa made of coquina stone plastered with lime-and-sand mortar. After the English occupation began in 1763, a second story was added onto the house beneath a hipped roof covered in wood shingles. One of St. Augustine's classic cantilevered wooden balconies hangs off the old walls. The wooden beams that support the porch project out over the street to hold up square posts and a hipped roof.

The Gonzalez-Alvarez House (fig. 15) is known in St. Augustine as the Oldest House, its Spanish walls built of coquina stone with a timber-frame second story added by the English. Typical of late eighteenth-century English construction, the upper walls are covered with beveled clapboards painted gray-green, making the Oldest House the perfect example of the city's fusion of Spanish and Anglo-Caribbean influences.

Drawing on these traditions from Florida's colonial era, a recent St. Augustine-style house has been designed on the Florida Panhandle by architect Jason Dunham (fig. 16). Dunham's house tips its hat to St. Augustine's layering of building traditions in a loose interpretation of old Spanish casas and West Indies plantation houses. The new house is tall and lanky, stretching sturdy Spanish masonry walls into slender stucco piers that march around the outside. This colonnade of white pillars supports a second story of airy, West Indies-style wooden porches.

Behind the stucco piers, the core of the house is a long rectangle of white stucco walls that enclose first-floor rooms. The walls are tall to match the height of the colonnade, with deep porches above made of square wooden posts filled in with plantation shutters painted dark spruce-green. A traditional shading device still used throughout the Caribbean, the shutters swing open to bring daylight and sea breezes into the second-floor bedrooms. These old ideas, reborn in the Florida Panhandle, create a new house that feels right at home.

Fig. 16. Rosemary Beach House, Jason Dunham, architect.

Fig. 17. Map of Louisiana Territory. W. Kemble. **Map of French, English, and Spanish Possessions in 1745.** *Published by Harper Brothers, New York, 1848. Engraving. Collection of Beaux Arts, Dallas.*

Fig. 18. A print showing typical French Colonial **poteaux-en-terre** *construction. George Henri Victor Collot.* **French Habitation in the Country of the Illinois.** *1826. Engraving. Yale Collection of Western Americana, Beinecke Rare Book and Manuscript Library, Yale University, New Haven, Connecticut.*

Gulf Coast Creole Cottage

"The Mississippi River towns are comely, clean, well built, and pleasing to the eye, and cheering to the spirit. The Mississippi Valley is as reposeful as dreamland, nothing worldly about it . . . nothing to hang a fret or worry upon."

—Mark Twain*, Life on the Mississippi* (1863)

Beginning in the early seventeenth century, the French settled North America in the St. Lawrence Valley, searching for sources of trade in furs, lumber, and minerals. Pushing deep into the interior of Canada, French *coureurs des bois* (woodsmen engaged in the fur trade) established trading posts with the native Indians around the Great Lakes. By the eighteenth century, their scattered forts and settlements along the inland waterways had become the cities of Montreal, Quebec, Detroit, Duluth, and St. Louis.

The French explorer René-Robert Cavelier de La Salle, lured by Indian tales of a great continental river, followed the Mississippi to its delta in 1682. Mapping everything he found, La Salle took French possession of the land he christened *La Louisiane* for King Louis XIV, including the entire Mississippi Valley, as well as the Missouri and Ohio river valleys. The prize was the founding of an international seaport in New Orleans in 1718.

By the start of the French and Indian War in 1754, France had laid claim to an enormous territory covering all of Canada and Louisiana, effectively encircling the English on the Atlantic coast and walling off New Spain to the south (fig. 17). The period of French ascendancy ended in 1763 when their colonial empire collapsed with the Treaty of Paris that concluded the Seven Years' War (America's French and Indian War). Thomas Jefferson's Louisiana Purchase from Napoleon in 1803 brought all of the Mississippi Valley under American control.

When the French first arrived in heavily wooded Acadia and Canada in the early 1600s, they improvised shelter by using logs to build walls of vertical posts set into trenches in the ground, called *poteaux-en-terre* (fig. 18). These palisades of vertical logs were chinked with clay to make them weather-tight and planked with split-board roofs.

Fig. 19. Jean Baptiste Bequette House, Ste. Genevieve, Missouri, 1793.

Toward the end of the seventeenth century, the French arrived in the Lower Mississippi Valley, with its hot and humid climate prone to seasonal flooding and hurricanes. To suit these new conditions, French settlers merged the cold-climate building traditions of French Canada with those of the French West Indies, creating the classic Creole cottage.

French colonial houses were built all along the Mississippi from the Great Lakes to the Gulf of Mexico. Almost none of the earliest French houses survive, but a splendid collection of somewhat later houses has been preserved in the town of Ste. Genevieve, Missouri. The house of Frenchman Jean Baptiste Bequette (fig. 19) is of classic poteaux-en-terre construction. Its vertical log walls are surrounded on four sides by gallery porches raised above ground on porch posts—a practice the French imported from the West Indies.

Designed for the subtropical Gulf Coast, the Creole houses of Louisiana were built of cypress timbers pegged together into rigid frames and raised above ground on piers. Their open web of timbers was filled in with *bousillage*, a thick mat of clay and moss, and then coated with lime plaster. Under a pavilion roof—a tent-like form that had been developed in the Caribbean—deep porches surrounded the house on all four sides, providing shelter from the sun and capturing cooling breezes.

*Fig. 20. Typical French Colonial **bousillage**
construction. Poche-Ezidore House, Gramercy,
Louisiana, early nineteenth century.*
.

Fig. 21. Cemetery House, Madisonville, Louisiana.

There is an original Creole cottage from the early 1800s in the town of
Gramercy, Louisiana, on the banks of the Mississippi. The Poche-Ezidore House
(fig. 20) is a raised cottage built of rustic cypress timbers with the spaces between
timbers filled in with bousillage. Later covered with horizontal clapboards, the
original walls are now exposed as part of a recent restoration.

Across Lake Pontchartrain from the port of New Orleans sits the sleepy Creole
town of Madisonville. There, restoration builder Ron Arnoult has recreated a
traditional Creole cottage with roots in French colonial architecture (fig. 21). Its
half-timbered walls resemble the medieval houses of coastal France that inspired
French colonists who settled in Canada. Blending the timber frame with porches
and a pavilion roof derived from the plantation houses of the French West Indies,
Arnoult has revived all the hallmarks of the classic Creole cottage.

The new home captures the true spirit of a raised cottage in its gallery-style
porches and pavilion roof that grace plantation houses all along Louisiana's River
Road. It is a single story and appears low and long, even though it is lifted several
feet above the ground on masonry piers. Raised foundations were a customary
architectural detail on early Creole cottages, allowing air to circulate under houses
to keep them cool and to prevent moisture from rotting the floor timbers. They
still work well today in the bayou country of Louisiana.

Fig. 22. Map of Spanish Texas. J. Yeager. **Texas, Mexico, and Part of the United States.** *1836. Philadelphia Print Shop.*

Spanish Mission Style

"When Texas is populated and governed by good laws, it will be one of the most enviable places in the world, in which it doubtless will play a brilliant role."
—José Enrique de la Peña, *La Rebelión de Texas* (1836)

The Spanish settled the borderlands of New Spain (Mexico) in the American Southwest beginning with the founding of Santa Fe in 1610. Spain's colonial outposts north of the border were principally fortified chains of presidios, missions, and pueblos, rather than pilgrim colonies. They relied on Dominican, Franciscan, and Jesuit missionaries to spread Spanish dominion, often settling in areas with established Indian populations to convert to Christianity.

Spanish Colonial architecture had evolved in New Spain for two centuries before it was transplanted to the north. In the borderlands, the Spaniards favored pragmatic construction over architectural display, largely because they were building in a primitive wilderness. The Spanish refined the mud-building techniques of the natives by stacking blocks of sun-dried adobe bricks into thick walls, beneath a mud-covered roof of crossed timbers and sticks. They introduced woodworking details for doors, windows, and carved decorative ornaments.

Fig. 23. Mission San Francisco de la Espada, San Antonio, Texas, 1740s–1750s.

In the 1690s, under threat from French settlements in the Mississippi Valley, the Spaniards reinforced New Spain's borderlands with a chain of missions across Texas (fig. 22). San Antonio—the mission cradle of Texas—began life in 1718 as the major presidio, or military garrison, and mission along the Camino Real, or Royal Road. Guided by Franciscan friars, Indian converts built mighty churches as fortress-like centerpieces for missions like the Alamo.

San Antonio boasts one of the greatest concentrations of Spanish missions in North America, with five missions arrayed in a chain that follows the San Antonio River south for ten miles. They were built close together for protection against Apache and Comanche Indian attacks and to share a common irrigation system. The missions were simplified versions of the Baroque cathedrals of New Spain, made of adobe or quarried limestone blocks and decorated with an expressive front door and an occasional mission belfry, called a *campanario*.

In the sun-parched Southwest, the Spanish perfected building stout mission walls for protection and insulation. They used arcades of half-round arches for covered porches and passageways. Windows were small, simple openings cut through the walls, designed to minimize heat intrusion and keep the interiors cool. Roofs were covered in mission tiles made of fired red clay shaped into half-round barrels.

The southernmost and most austere mission in the chain is Mission San Francisco de la Espada (fig. 23). Espada's sober facade resembles a giant tombstone

Fig. 24. Mission San José y San Miguel de Aquayo, San Antonio, Texas, 1768–82.

Fig. 25. Rancho dos Vidas, Michael Imber, architect.

made of rough Texas rubble, called tufa, mortared together with lime. The top of the wall is a tiered espadaña with bells suspended in three cutout arches. Mission San José y San Miguel de Aquayo (fig. 24), known as the "Queen of the Missions," is a classic Roman cross church with a dome like the Renaissance cathedrals of Europe. Its elaborate frontispiece is a sixteenth-century Spanish design dripping with ornament and carved figures of the saints, probably executed by sculptors from Mexico City.

Inspired by the bell towers and red clay tile roofs of the Texas missions, architect Michael Imber has created a new ranch called Rancho dos Vidas in the mesquite and sagebrush savannah south of San Antonio (fig. 25). Its mission-style walls enclose a hacienda buttressed against a hillside like a fortified Spanish presidio built in a wild landscape setting as a self-sufficient oasis.

Like an old Spanish mission, the ranch is a string of building parts clustered together into a compound of living rooms, bedrooms, kitchen, and garage that form a courtyard enclosed within high walls. Its stucco walls, stained the color of poached salmon, shelter the house in the hardscrabble landscape. The thick masonry walls absorb the Texas heat, promising cool sanctuary inside, while windows and doors are deeply recessed to shade them from the sun. To this day, these essential features of mission architecture offer appropriate ways to deal with the harsh climate of South Texas.

Texas-German Rock House
"The German emigrants who came to the hill country of South-Central Texas . . .
gave the land an identifying mark by erecting structures that combine traditional
German influences . . . in houses and service buildings constructed of half-timbering
or rock-and-mortar methods of local limestone."
—Hubert Wilhelm, *German Settlement on the Frontier of South-Central Texas* (1968)

The gentle hills and valleys that rise northwest of San Antonio are home to a unique Texas subculture known as the Hill Country. The landscape is laced with small towns and ranches that border the Medina, Guadalupe, and Pedernales rivers. This was Indian territory in Spanish Texas before scores of European immigrants came to settle here in the 1830s. There is a distinctive German flavor to the Hill Country, preserved in foothills first settled by pioneers in the early nineteenth century.

*Fig. 26. Alfred Henke House,
Fredericksburg, Texas,
mid-nineteenth century.*

*Fig. 27. Carl Wilhelm Rummel House,
Round Top, Texas, c. 1870.*

*Fig. 28. Typical Sunday House,
Fredericksburg, Texas.*

Following the Texas Revolution of 1836, President Sam Houston of the newly minted Republic of Texas sent out a call to Europe for settlers to come populate his new dominions, luring them to the frontier with generous grants of land. Driven from their farms by bitter cold winters, failing crops, overcrowding, and exorbitant prices in 1830s Europe, German pioneers heeded the call and came to make a fresh start in Texas.

They came from Hesse, the Rhineland, and Lower Saxony in Germany, as well as from Alsace in France. The verdant Hill Country west of San Antonio beckoned with wide-open meadows, live oaks and cedars, limestone soils, and abundant water. Peasant farmers soon imprinted the landscape of the Hill Country with a unique personality colored by German and Alsatian traditions in towns like New Braunfels, Castroville, Comfort, and Fredericksburg.

Examples of well-preserved German houses abound across the Texas Hill Country. While they first built houses of log, they then tried *Fachwerk*, a form of timber framing where a skeleton of timber posts and beams was filled in with adobe bricks or stones and whitewashed. But the industrious Germans craved more permanent homes, and at the first flush of prosperity replaced logs and *Fachwerk* with stone (fig. 26).

With every hillside ledge offering soft and easily workable Texas limestone, craftsmen revived old Rhineland Valley masonry traditions to build farmhouses of cut stone, creating what became known as the Texas "rock house." During the late nineteenth century, their house forms began to resemble the American Federal and Greek Revival styles, featuring two-story gables and symmetrical patterns for windows and doors. German and American traditions blended seamlessly into a new Texas style. The 1870 Carl Wilhelm Rummel House (fig. 27) in Round Top shows a Texas rock house with a classic front porch and supporting columns. The Johann Traugott Wandke House (1863), also in Round Top, looks like a distant cousin of a Pennsylvania Dutch farmhouse covered by a steep roof with a sturdy stone chimney.

The Hill Country Germans also built small but distinctive Sunday Houses (fig. 28) as in-town weekend retreats, places where ranchers could attend church, go shopping, and socialize with neighbors while taking a break from the outback. Early Sunday Houses were built of *Fachwerk* or limestone rock, with one large room warmed by a fireplace and a porch built across the front to welcome visitors.

Fig. 29. John Peter Tatsch Barn, Fredericksburg, Texas, 1852.

Fig. 30. Misty Hills Ranch, Ignacio Salas-Humara, architect.

Texas Germans even adopted the saltbox shape, a familiar form from the New England colonies. The barn of John Peter Tatsch in Fredericksburg (fig. 29) is a saltbox type made of vertical boards over a timber frame with wooden battens covering the butt joints between boards.

In the heart of the Hill Country's Medina Valley, a new ranch called Misty Hills commands a hilltop site overlooking river bottomland (fig. 30). Designed by architect Ignacio Salas-Humara, the house captures the region's country roots shaped in walls of mellow Texas limestone, vintage timbers, and rusted metal roofs. The house is a field guide to historic architecture from the region's German, Alsatian, and American pasts.

At its heart, the new ranch is a Sunday House on steroids with many classic features rendered in super size. Attached to the house is a collection of historic artifacts—a log cabin, wagon barn, bunkhouse, and water tower—strung together in a rambling residence. Some of the parts are salvaged buildings, like a nineteenth-century dogtrot log cabin, while others are authentic re-creations built of old materials. Misty Hills Ranch leaves no doubt that this is a new house with deep roots in Texas's past.

Roots of Home—A Living Legacy

The story of the architecture of the South and of Texas is just one chapter in the American journey. There are many other regional tales of colonial trailblazers who populated the New World with their building traditions and transformed them into distinctly American styles.

Our architectural legacy begins with these journeys across time but does not end there. The adventure has taken new twists and turns over four centuries as classic styles have evolved and changed. Time and again, we have returned fondly to the classics as we build new cities, towns, and suburbs across the continent. And a new chapter is being written again today, by architects who are creating new "old" houses to suit life in the modern age. For inspiration, they are returning to the same living traditions that hold the precious seeds of our past—the roots of home.

TREE OF TEXAS PAINTING

Romanticism Goes West: Nineteenth-Century European Painters in Texas

Sam Ratcliffe

In the 1930s or early 1940s, Dallas artist and art critic Jerry Bywaters attempted to distill the history of painting in Texas into a single drawing, *The Tree of Texas
Painting* (fig. 1). Although the work is undated, Bywaters likely drew inspiration
from Miguel Covarrubias's "Tree of Modern Art," published in *Vanity Fair* in May
1933. The tree is flanked on one side by a depiction of a Plains Indian encampment and notations regarding Trans-Pecos pictographs and petroglyphs left by
the region's earliest inhabitants, and on the other by a rendering of San Antonio's
Mission Concepción. The rest of the drawing brings in virtually every strain of the
state's painting, from "Cattle Painters" to "Internationalists" and "Abstractionists."
Bywaters added a touch of humor by portraying the sometimes controversial Davis
Wildflower Competitions during the 1920s at San Antonio's Witte Museum as a
hornet's nest. Bywaters portrays European immigrant painters of the early and mid-
1800s as comprising the "roots" of Texas painting. Now, some seventy years later,
these roots provide a focal point for this paper examining the work of artists who
emigrated to Texas from Europe, according to their respective nations of origin.[1]

While the term "Romanticism" provides a convenient umbrella for describing
these artists, it refers as much to the time period in which they worked as to the

Fig. 1. Jerry Bywaters. Tree of Texas Painting. *n.d. Pencil on paper, 21
x 16 in. (53.4 x 40.6 cm). Jerry Bywaters Collection on Art of the
Southwest, Hamon Arts Library, Southern Methodist University, Dallas.*

Fig. 2. Unknown photographer. **Portrait of Thomas**
Flintoff. *c. 1860–65. Albumen silver carte-de-visite,*
4 1/4 x 2 1/2 in. (10.7 x 6.5 cm). State Library of
Victoria, Australia (H10668).

Fig. 3. Thomas Flintoff. **Portrait of the Jones**
Children of Galveston. *c. 1852. Oil on canvas,*
56 3/4 x 42 7/16 in. (144.1 x 107.8 cm).
The Bayou Bend Collection, gift of Miss Ima Hogg
(B.59.132).

philosophy of each artist. Some of them, such as Richard Petri and Hermann
Lungkwitz, clearly worked in that tradition, while its manifestation in the works of
others, such as Theodore Gentilz, is not as pervasive. By the mid-nineteenth century, Romanticism had touched Europeans' perceptions of the American frontier and
its native peoples. For example, almost immediately after attaining widespread popularity in the United States, the Leatherstocking novels of James Fenimore Cooper
were being translated into several European languages. This fascination included
idealizing America's native tribes as Stoic philosophers living in harmony with Nature
in an egalitarian, democratic utopia; some visitors from Europe hoped that the
Indian's "example" somehow could serve as a reform mechanism for European cities
that were falling prey to the problems of urbanization and worker discontent
accompanying the Industrial Revolution. Most artists who came to Texas were of
the European educated class and held at least some of its predominant attitudes
towards the native peoples of the New World.[2]

Although English was the native tongue of the majority of nineteenth-century
Texas immigrants, relatively few painters from the British Isles worked in the state.

*Fig. 4. Thomas Flintoff. **Catholic Church, Houston, Texas**. 1852.*
Watercolor, 10 x 14 in. (25.4 x 35.6 cm). The Bayou Bend Collection,
gift of Cynthia and Tony Petrello in honor of Carena Petrello at "One
Great Night in November, 2007" (B.2007.9).

Thomas Flintoff (c. 1809–1891) (fig. 2), an itinerant portrait painter who was
born in Newcastle-upon-Tyne, England, emigrated to the United States around
1850. Though little is known of his early life, the fact that he had received some
training is evident in his work, for his paintings show that he had at least been
exposed to the elements of English Romantic style. However, at this stage of his
career, Flintoff's work is somewhat primitive, occasionally showing a lack of skill
in rendering depth and painting detail. He arrived in Texas in the spring of 1851,
hoping to be hired to execute portraits of newly prosperous planters and business-
men and their families (fig. 3). Later that year, Flintoff traveled to Austin, where
he was commissioned by the legislature to restore its portrait of Stephen F. Austin.[3]

In the spring of 1852, Flintoff visited Houston, Indianola (subsequently
destroyed by a hurricane), and Matagorda (figs. 4–6). He recorded his impressions
of these towns in a series of watercolor sketches that are invaluable to historians.
Many of them depict municipal buildings and churches that were demolished later
in the nineteenth century and would otherwise have been known only by written
descriptions. Flintoff left Texas in 1852 and joined other members of his family

Fig. 5. Thomas Flintoff. **Indianola, Texas, and Indianola with Lavaca Point in the Distance.** 1852. Watercolor, 10 7/16 x 13 7/8 in. (26.5 x 35.2 cm). The Bayou Bend Collection, gift of Lee Godfrey in honor of his wife, Sandy Godfrey, at "One Great Night in November, 2007" (B.2007.10).

Fig. 6. Thomas Flintoff. **Masonic Hall, Matagorda, Texas.** 1852. Watercolor. 10 3/4 x 14 3/8 in. (27.3 x 36.5 cm). The Bayou Bend Collection, gift of Henry J. N. Taub II in honor of Paul Hobby at "One Great Night in November, 2007" (B.2007.8).

Fig. 7. Thomas Flintoff.
Sir William John Clark, Baronet. 1885. Oil on
canvas. 58 7/8 x 46 3/4 in. (149.5 x 118.8 cm).
State Library of Victoria, Australia (H141877).

Fig. 8. Henry A. McArdle.
The Settlement of Austin's Colony. 1875. Oil on
canvas, 83 1/4 x 60 1/2 in. (211.5 x 153.7 cm).
The State Preservation Board, Austin, Texas.

who had migrated to Melbourne, Australia, where he became a noted portrait
painter before his death in 1891 (fig. 7).[4]

In contrast to Flintoff's brief stay in Texas, Henry Arthur McArdle lived in the
state for many years after moving from Virginia. McArdle, a native of Ireland, had
emigrated to Baltimore with an aunt at the age of fifteen and studied at the
Maryland Institute for the Promotion of the Mechanic Arts, graduating in 1860.
He put his artistic abilities to use for the Confederate Army, including serving as
one of the topographical artists on the staff of General Robert E. Lee. Following
the war, he joined the art faculty of Baylor Female College in Independence, Texas,
in 1867. While painting portraits of veterans of the Texas Revolution, McArdle
became intrigued by their stories of Texas history. In 1874, Major Moses Austin
Bryan, Stephen F. Austin's nephew, suggested that the artist immortalize Austin's
role in bringing Anglo settlers to Texas. McArdle envisioned *The Settlement of Austin's
Colony* (fig. 8), also known as *The Log Cabin*, as the first of a series of works in
"which I hope to illustrate to posterity the grand achievements of the heroes and

*Fig. 9. Henry A. McArdle, **Dawn at the Alamo**. 1905. Oil on canvas, 84 x 144 in. (213.4 x 365.8 cm). The State Preservation Board, Austin, Texas.*

statesmen of the Texas Revolution." Although the title of the painting does not link it to a particular event, McArdle's brief explanation in his scrapbooks at the Texas State Archives indicates that he had in mind Austin's campaign against the Karankawas in the late summer of 1824.[5]

In 1875, McArdle completed *Dawn at the Alamo*, intending it to follow *The Settlement of Austin's Colony* in his proposed series of paintings depicting Texas heroes. McArdle loaned *Dawn at the Alamo* to the state and it was on exhibit in the Capitol when destroyed by the 1881 fire; this image now exists only in the form of a photographic reproduction. Over the next three decades, McArdle became obsessed with incorporating changes into a revised rendering of the battle scene that he hoped would improve his chances of selling it to the state. The revised *Dawn at the Alamo* (1905) (fig. 9), attempted to capture the entire sweep of the hand-to-hand combat during the climactic moments of the Revolution's most celebrated battle. McArdle corresponded with several individuals whom he regarded as experts on the battle, including Santa Anna and Reuben Potter, military historian of the Texas Revolution. The former Mexican leader, writing shortly before his death, justified his actions at the Alamo to McArdle on the grounds of the "obstinacy" of he "insulting" Travis and his men and by his own fear of Sam Houston's imminent arrival with a "respectable" amount of troops.[6]

Fig. 10. Henry A. McArdle. **Battle of San Jacinto.** *1895. Oil on canvas,*
96 x 168 in. (243.8 x 426.7 cm). The State Preservation Board, Austin, Texas.

McArdle depicted the results of Santa Anna's encounter with Houston's
"respectable" amount of troops in *The Battle of San Jacinto* (1895) (fig. 10). Set on
an open battlefield rather than in an enclosed fort, this work furnished McArdle
with an even better opportunity than did *Dawn at the Alamo* to display the skills
that he had honed as a topographical artist. He accurately depicted Houston as
attempting to continue to lead the Texan charge after having had his horse shot
from under him and his right ankle shattered by a musket ball. In the center left
portion of the canvas, beside a Mexican battery, the Texan commander waves his
white planter's hat as he prepares to lead his men afoot against a small band of
riflemen forming behind Mexican General Manuel Fernandez Castrillon. By
contrast, in the painting's upper right portion, Santa Anna, mounted on a black
horse and wearing a white sombrero, flees the battlefield. A brown mule, trailing a
rope from his neck, races behind him while a black mule kicks his hind legs into
the air before the fleeing "Napoleon of the West." McArdle explained that he had
included this prosaic vignette to demonstrate that "even [Santa Anna's] mules have
lost respect for him."[7]

But McArdle's depictions of Mexican combatants also included a number
of portrayals of courage. For example, Reuben Potter designated Captain Juan
Seguin's small force of Tejanos as "the only contingent of native Texans," and other

Fig. 11. Theodore Gentilz. **Surveying in Texas Before Annexation to U.S. (Stick Stock).** *1845. Oil on canvas, 7 x 9 1/2 in. (17.8 x 24.1 cm). Collection of Mr. and Mrs. Larry Sheerin, San Antonio, Texas.*

prominent Texans asked McArdle to emphasize this detachment's heroism.[8] Bravery shown by soldiers of both sides unifies the many discrete and simultaneous vignettes on the canvas, such as Antonio Trevino and Henry Karnes engaged in mounted combat for possession of a Mexican flag (lower right corner) and General Castrillon's attempt to rally a semblance of resistance (center right portion). A key motivation for McArdle's timing of work on this painting—which meant interrupting revision of *Dawn at the Alamo*—was the opportunity to interview and correspond with veterans and their families in order to be able to execute the canvas in their lifetimes.[9]

McArdle was careful to situate the viewer on an elevation facing northeastward across the battlefield, looking away from the setting sun. He hoped that the shadows of sunset would "add to the dramatic effect of the death-grapple" and convey "intense

Fig. 12. Theodore Gentilz. **Camp of the Lipans.** 1896. Oil on canvas, 9 x 12 in. (22.9 x 30.5 cm).
Courtesy of the Witte Museum, San Antonio, Texas.

and graphic power softened by poetic fervour."[10] In the final section of his description
of the painting, entitled "Freedom's Light: Triumph of Texas' Independence (The
aspect of the Heavens)," McArdle elaborated on his manipulation of clouds and
sunlight: "Dark, inauspicious, and threatening clouds which overspread the heavens
are suggestive of the suffering, danger, and death. under which Texas had struggled . . .
last rays of the setting sun break through the gloom, typical of the light and freedom
and victory which is to be the result of the Texian victory at San Jacinto."[11]

French painter Theodore Gentilz (1819–1906) similarly utilized interviews
with contemporaries of historical events in his depictions of Texas scenes. Gentilz
was educated at L'École Impériale de Mathématiques et de Dessin in his native
Paris, studying with René Monvoisin, and emigrated to Texas in 1844 to serve as

Fig. 13. Theodore Gentilz. **Death of Dickinson.** *c. 1890. Oil on canvas, 8 1/2 x 14 in. (21.6 x 35.6 cm). Yanaguana Society Collection, The Daughters of The Republic of Texas Library, San Antonio.*

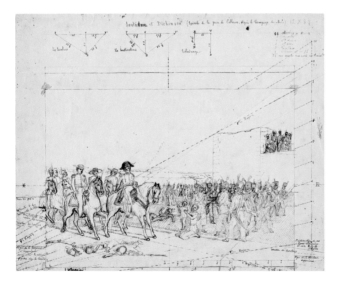

Fig.14. Theodore Gentilz. **Santa Anna et Dickinson.** *n.d. Pen and ink with pencil, 8 1/4 x 12 in. (21 x 30.5 cm). Gentilz-Fretelliere Family Papers, 80/15, The Daughters of The Republic of Texas Library (SC889.80.15).*

Fig. 15. Theodore Gentilz, **Corrida de la Sandia**, *n.d. Oil on canvas, 9 x 12 in. (22.9 x 30.5 cm). Yanaguana Society Collection, The Daughters of The Republic of Texas Library, San Antonio.*

artist and chief engineer for French colonizer Henri Castro. One of his first paintings in Texas depicted the artist working in his official capacity during the survey of the future site of the town of Castroville, late in the summer of 1844. The artist's portrayal of himself sighting down the surveyor's line near the center of the painting explains his titling of the work, *Surveying in Texas Before Annexation to U.S. (Stick Stock)* (1845) (fig. 11). Three years after this survey, Gentilz returned to Europe to recruit settlers for Castroville in Antwerp. In the first months of 1848, he moved back to Texas and lived out his life in San Antonio, embracing what he perceived as all of the exotic elements of the history and life of his adopted land.[12]

Gentilz's *Camp of the Lipans* (1896) (fig. 12) resulted from his work as a surveyor that had brought him into contact with members of Texas Indian tribes. This painting has a somewhat elegiac quality, due perhaps in part to the fact that Gentilz executed it a half century after his surveying duties were over. In the foreground, an Indian youth aims an arrow at an unseen fish and a mother restrains her child from wading into the stream. In the background, Gentilz's Indians are involved in the daily activities of any community: pairs of individuals are engaged in conversation, a woman sits beside her cooking fire, and, behind the young archer, an apprehensive father stands by, watching his child demonstrate an ability to ride a horse bareback. In these paintings, each of which constitutes a small story, Gentilz depicted Indians forthrightly and avoided the extremes of "Nature's noblemen" or "blood-thirsty savages."

Within a year of his return to Texas, Gentilz had begun sketching the San Antonio missions and interviewing San Antonians in order to obtain details of the siege of the Alamo that he could later include in such works as *Death of Dickinson* (fig. 13). His studies and preliminary sketches reflect detailed research down to the level of depiction of such elements as bridle bits and knives. Especially interesting is a sketch of the scene replete with Gentilz's lines of perspective that illustrates how he handled the painting as a mathematical construction, placing the figure of Captain Almeron Dickinson within a triangle formed by the horsemen and buildings and conveying the effect of the figures' shadows continuing beyond the edge of the canvas (fig. 14).[13]

Gentilz's depiction of Dickinson pleading for his life by holding aloft his young daughter, who clutches a white flag, runs counter to most accounts of Dickinson's death, including that given by Susannah Dickinson. She recalled that, as the third assault breached the walls, she had lifted up her daughter to Captain Dickinson for one final embrace shortly before he died with the other members of the garrison.[14] Choosing to disagree with this generally accepted version of Dickinson's death, Gentilz drew his idea for the painting from the recollections of Antonio Cruz Arrocha, a resident of San Antonio at the time of the siege. Arrocha maintained that, following the battle, Dickinson appeared from a hiding place carrying his child, who held a white flag, and knelt before Santa Anna as the Mexican commander approached the chapel. Showing no mercy, Santa Anna allegedly ordered his hesitant infantrymen to bayonet the pair.[15] Despite the subject matter of this work, Gentilz clearly regarded the Alamo in conventional nineteenth-century Texan fashion, as indicated in his brief summary of its history in the margin of one of his sketches, which repeated Texans' frequent equation of the Alamo battle with the massacre of King Leonidas's Spartan army in 480 B.C. This notation declared that "Travis, Bowie, Crockett, and their noble companion martyrs defied Santana [sic] and the Mexican army and enacted the tragedy which gives the Alamo the name of the 'Thermopylae of America.'"[16]

*Fig. 16. Eugénie Aubanel Lavender. **Still Life with Game Birds**. 1892. Oil on canvas, 18 x 25 in. (45.7 x 63.5 cm). Courtesy of the Witte Museum, San Antonio, Texas.*

*Fig. 17. Louise Heuser Wueste. **Eliza Busen Wueste**, n.d. Pencil, 10 x 8 3/16 in. (20.4 x 20.8 cm). Jerry Bywaters Collection on Art of the Southwest, Hamon Arts Library, Southern Methodist University.*

*Fig. 18. Louise Heuser Wueste. **Peter Wilhelm Leopold Wueste**, n.d. 14 1/2 x 11 1/4 in. (36.8 x 28.6 cm). Courtesy of the Witte Museum, San Antonio, Texas.*

Fig. 19. Carl G. von Iwonski. **Log Cabin, New Braunfels.** *c. 1853. Oil on canvas, 8 1/2 x 11 1/2 in. (21.6 x 29.2 cm). Yanaguana Society Collection, The Daughters of The Republic of Texas Library.*

Even more than the Alamo, Gentilz was intrigued with Hispanic life in his adopted city, portraying a variety of activities associated with everyday life, as in *Corrida de la Sandia* (fig. 15). Gentilz's sketches indicate that many of these works were set in specific places in San Antonio, as he included architectural details and noted the names of streets around the borders of the images. Gentilz plotted these works with the same mathematical precision that he devoted to more "monumental" subjects, such as the Alamo, making complicated notes concerning lines of perspective and use of color in his intricate study sketches.[17]

Another French immigrant painter, Eugénie Aubanel Lavender (1817–1898), studied at Paris's École de Beaux-Arts under Paul Delaroche and other popular painters in the Romantic Realist tradition. Her studies at the school included painting historical pictures, portraits, and copying famous paintings in the Louvre, and her work received recognition commensurate with that given to her fellow student Rosa Bonheur, subsequently one of France's most famous painters. In 1846, Eugénie married Charles Lavender, a professor at the University of Paris and the son of a London lithographer. In 1852, in the face of protests from both sets of

Fig. 20. Carl G. von Iwonski. **Sam Maverick and the Terry Rangers.** *c. 1862. Oil on canvas, 11 1/2 x 15 in. (29.2 x 38.1 cm). Courtesy of the Witte Museum, San Antonio, Texas.*

parents, the couple and their two children crossed the Atlantic, landing in New Orleans. This was their "jumping-off point" for a trek via prairie schooner across southeastern Texas before finally settling in Waco, where their two daughters played with the little boy next door, Lawrence Sullivan Ross, later a legendary Texas Ranger captain. Mrs. Lavender hunted with a rifle, carried a pistol and a knife, and wore deerskin and a large wide-brimmed hat. According to their granddaughter, "the vastness of the Texas prairies, the wildness of their surroundings, and the novelty of it all satisfied to a certain extent their yen for a romantic life in Nature."[18] However, after two years, they moved from Waco to New Orleans. Following her husband's death in the late 1870s, Eugénie Lavender moved to Corpus Christi to live with her daughter, where she painted *Still Life with Game Birds* (fig. 16). The seventy-five year-old Mrs. Lavender was perhaps refocusing on her early training at the École des Beaux-Arts and the Louvre, employing such elements of Romantic Realism as exotic game birds surrounded by drapery and foliage viewed against the backdrop of an idealized landscape in the distance.[19]

Fig. 21. Carl G. von Iwonski. **Theater at Old Casino Club in San Antonio**. c. 1858–60. Oil on canvas, 9 1/2 x 14 in. (24.1 x 36.6 cm). Courtesy of the Witte Museum, San Antonio, Texas.

Fig. 22. Johan Christian Dahl. **Ship Stranded on the Norwegian Coast**. 1832. Oil on canvas, 28 1/8 x 43 3/4 in. (71.5 x 111 cm). The National Museum of Art, Architecture, and Design, the National Gallery, Oslo (NG.M.01626).

The other woman artist considered here—and the first of several German artists—is Louise Heuser Wueste (1805–1874). She studied at the Dusseldorf Royal Academy and two of her sisters had married prominent German artists, who encouraged Louise and helped her with her painting. She immigrated to Texas at the age of fifty-four, settling with her children in San Antonio, where she taught sewing and, possibly, drawing at the German-English School in the La Villita neighborhood. She executed portraits of family members, such as these of her husband and daughter-in-law (figs. 17–18), and supplemented her income by painting portraits of other residents of the city.[20]

Another prominent member of San Antonio's community of German artists, Carl G. von Iwonski (1830–1912), emigrated to Texas with his family in 1846 from his native Silesia, a province at various times part of both Germany and Poland. *Log Cabin, New Braunfels* (c. 1853) (fig. 19) portrayed his family's farm in Guadalupe (later Comal) County. But most of his early paintings depicted the activities of the German Theatre group of New Braunfels in the mid-1850s. In 1857 or 1858, Iwonski moved to San Antonio and, although he lacked extensive formal artistic training, began retouching portraits in oil and other media in the studio of William DeRyee, a pioneer chemist and photographer from Bavaria.[21]

At the outbreak of hostilities in 1861, Iwonski was teaching in San Antonio's German-American school and openly opposed secession. Ironically, Iwonski's accurately detailed sketch of a Confederate encampment near San Antonio was the first illustration of the war to appear in *Harper's Weekly*.[22] He also executed one of the few paintings of Texan Confederate soldiers' activities in the state. *The Terry Rangers* (c. 1862) (fig. 20), also titled *Sam Maverick and the Terry Rangers*, portrays the son of a pioneer citizen of San Antonio departing the city after enlisting as a private in the Confederate Army in the spring of 1862. Young Maverick joined the 8th Texas Cavalry, commanded by B. F. Terry, which became one of the most famous Texas units to fight in the Civil War. Iwonski and the Maverick family apparently "agreed to disagree" concerning the war in order for one of the city's foremost artists and illustrators to render this portrayal.[23]

Following the war, Iwonski and German artist Hermann Lungkwitz (1813–1891) opened a painting and photography studio. Most of Iwonski's artistic subjects in San Antonio consisted of portraits and cultural events, such as the activities of the city's Casino Club, a center of cultural activities and dramatic arts (fig. 21). His choice of subjects, aside from those of his portraits, indicates that Iwonski felt less com-

*Fig. 23. Hermann Lungkwitz. **Enchanted Rock.** 1864. Oil on canvas mounted on panel, 14 x 20 in. (36.6 x 50.8 cm). Courtesy of the Witte Museum, San Antonio, Texas.*

fortable in a rural, frontier setting than did other European artists in Texas and, indeed, he moved back to Germany following its unification in 1871.[24]

Iwonski's studio partner, Hermann Lungkwitz, had artistic roots in the late Romantic tradition of Dresden, where he studied at the Academy of Fine Arts between 1840 and 1843. The Romantic movement had a primarily artistic and literary focus but also was linked closely to a growing sense of political nationalism and unrest. By 1848, this drive for political change had touched off riots in Dresden, in which Lungkwitz participated alongside fellow art student Friedrich Richard Petri, his future brother-in-law. As the revolution failed, the family decided to immigrate to Texas. The Lungkwitz-Petri family arrived late in 1851 in New Braunfels and, in July 1852, settled on a farm five miles southwest of Fredericksburg, a six-year-old village of five hundred people.[25]

The German Romanticism that suffused Lungkwitz's academic training and that influenced his landscape painting in Germany as well as in the United States emphasized human insignificance in the face of an awe-inspiring natural world and, in Europe, the revival of interest in ancient epics, medieval themes, and Renaissance German and Nordic history. In Dresden, Lungkwitz studied most directly under

Fig. 24. Hermann Lungkwitz. **Hill Country Landscape.** *1862. Oil on canvas. 18 3/8 x 23 13/16 in. (46.7 x 60.5 cm). The Bayou Bend Collection, gift of Miss Ima Hogg (B.67.39).*

Ludwig Richter but also would have had some contact with the Norwegian Johan Christian Dahl (1788–1857). Dahl's teaching stressed naturalistic landscape painting (fig. 22), perhaps explaining why Lungkwitz's art evidences relatively little influence of the metaphysical and mystical approach of the most prominent north German romantic painter, Caspar David Friedrich.[26]

Lungkwitz's realistic interpretation of nature arose from his personal inclination as well as academic training. Notations on his study sketches indicate that he frequently worked out of doors during the late summer and early fall. His European drawings particularly reflect Lungkwitz's practice of giving the greatest attention to the composition's central element, while lightly sketching in background elements for fuller treatment later in his studio, along with the borders of the composition. Both in Germany and in Texas, Lungkwitz utilized rocks more than any other single compositional element, and Enchanted Rock, near Fredericksburg, proved to be his favorite subject (figs. 23–24). The study and finished version of *West Cave on the Pedernales* demonstrates Lungkwitz's skills in fine-line pencil or pen drawings from nature and also captures the overwhelming solitude and power of nature, as did many of his other works from the 1870s and 1880s (figs. 25–26). Although Lungkwitz showed

Fig. 25. Hermann Lungkwitz. **West Cave on the Pedernales.** *1880. Pencil,
11 1/2 x 17 3/8 in. (29.2 x 44.1 cm).William Hill Land & Cattle Company.*

Fig. 26. Hermann Lungkwitz. **West Cave on the Pedernales.** *1883.
Oil on canvas. 18 1/2 x 23 1/2 in. (47 x 59.7 cm). William Hill Land & Cattle Company.*

relatively little interest in orthodox religion, rocks in the Romantic mindset symbolized faith. Unlike Richter, Lungkwitz used human or other figures sparingly in his pictures, so it is ironic that in one of his best-known paintings, *Crockett Street Looking West*, the viewer's eye focuses on one of Lungkwitz's rare figures (fig. 27). As in other scenes, Lungkwitz's academic training enabled him to bring together draftsmanship and a painterliness to draw the viewer in along a street—or, in other works, down a stream or a valley—as he arranged the foreground, middle-ground, and background planes. These paintings certainly justify the only known evaluation of Lungkwitz from a German source, a 1908 catalogue for an exhibition of Dresden painters from the first half of the nineteenth century, as one of the "promising new talents" who was lost to his homeland because of the revolution of 1848–49.[27]

By contrast, Friedrich Richard Petri (1824–1857) populated a large number of his works with human subjects. Although he had painted extensively in oils during his student days at Dresden, Petri seems to have later worked primarily in watercolor (fig. 28). *Fort Martin Scott*, his only known attempt at oil painting in Texas, serves as a useful document of individuals active on this portion of the Texas frontier during the 1850s (fig. 29). For example, Major James Longstreet, the uniformed officer in the center of the painting, went on to a Civil War career as a famous Confederate general. The identity of the unpainted figure of an Indian woman in *Fort Martin Scott* is a mystery, although Petri had previously painted a similar portrait on another canvas and identified the subject as a Lipan Apache. In the spring of 1853, several Lipans were brought to the fort, located two miles east of Fredericksburg, for negotiations with military authorities, and this Indian woman may well have been a member of that group. Depictions of other Indians in the painting reflect Petri's sense of humor: the cherubic Indian child, whose torn shirt at first glance resembles wings, crawls into the midst of this gathering while an Indian boy emerges from his tent in the lower left to wrestle with a dog for a bone. Of course, this last element is two-edged, possibly illustrating Petri's disgust with the fact that Plains Indians had been reduced to such depths in order to eat.[28]

Petri captured the stern pride of Lipan Apache and Penateka Comanche warriors in works such as *Plains Indian Warrior in Blue* (fig. 30), the first depiction by a white artist of the hair-pipe breastplate and silver pendant characteristic of the costume of Penateka Comanche warriors. This painting also illustrated these tribes' practices of facial and body painting and of male ornamentation. Petri's warriors in these and other canvases stand as representative "noble savages" who would have incarnated the expectations of the most romantic European.[29]

Fig. 27. Hermann Lungkwitz. **Crockett Street Looking West, San Antonio**. 1857. Oil on canvas mounted on panel, 13 x 20 in. (33 x 50.8 cm). Courtesy of the Witte Museum, San Antonio, Texas.

Fig. 28. Friedrich Petri. **Campfire Scene**. n.d. Watercolor, 6 1/2 x 4 58 in. (16.5 x 11.7 cm). The University of Texas at Austin, Dolph Briscoe Center for American History.

Fig. 29. Friedrich Petri. **Fort Martin Scott**. c. 1853. Oil on canvas, 16 3/4 x 23 1/4 in.
(42.5 x 59 cm). The University of Texas at Austin, Dolph Briscoe Center for American History.

Despite Petri's skill in portraying warriors, these works do not represent the only
subject of his Indian paintings. Instead, Petri was drawn to these men as they participated in the daily life of their tribe and he depicted them within that context. In
Indian Family Emerging from the Woods (fig. 31), Petri emphasized the importance of
the institution of the family in Lipan and Comanche culture, implying the similarity
of this culture to that of white settlers. Petri's devotion to members of his own family
is evident in their many portraits, and two of the artist's most charming works
portrayed life on his family's farm. *In Pioneer Cowpen* (fig. 32), Petri again exhibited
an eye for humorous, realistic detail as a hen catches ticks near one of the cows and a
calf nuzzles Marie Petri, the artist's sister, while she is milking. Petri also took care to
render architectural details of the buildings, the curtains fluttering in the window,
and cattle brands, a New World novelty that intrigued him. Hermann Lungkwitz
rides across the yard in the background of the painting. *Going Visiting* (fig. 33),
portraying the family in formal dress—complete with parasols—points out that not
all Texas settlers lived in a totally primitive or rude environment. In this painting,
Petri depicted himself guiding the ox team that pulled the wagon bearing the rest
of the family. The local mill, the site of much of the social and business life of
many nineteenth-century Texas communities, stands in the background.[30]

*Fig. 30. Friedrich Petri. **Plains Indian Warrior in Blue**. n.d. Watercolor, 6 1/2 x 4 5/8 in. (16.5 x 11.7 cm). The University of Texas at Austin, Dolph Briscoe Center for American History.*

*Fig. 31. Friedrich Petri. **Indian Family Emerging from the Woods**. n.d. Watercolor, 4 x 6 in. (10.2 x 15.2 cm). The University of Texas at Austin, Dolph Briscoe Center for American History.*

The Petri-Lungkwitz family typified the overwhelming majority of all Texas settlers; living an undramatic existence engaged in mostly agricultural pursuits, their lives seemed to confirm the aspirations that Stephen F. Austin had held for Texas as an ideal haven for farmers. To sell their produce and obtain goods, many of these families depended on the port of Galveston.

German immigrant Julius Stockfleth (1857–1935) was the only professional painter to depict the Texas Gulf Coast in Galveston's heyday. At age 26, Stockfleth followed his family in immigrating to Lake Charles, Louisiana. Two years later, the Stockfleths moved to Galveston, where Julius worked as a painter for the next twenty-two years. Although an apprenticeship to a village painter had been his only professional training before coming to America, Stockfleth painted numerous scenes of Galveston's bustling harbor in addition to portraits, landscapes, and architectural studies of Galveston residences (fig. 34).[31] The artist viewed his role as that of a "topographical documentarian" of maritime shipping, working in a genre of painting that demanded depictions of ships and harbor life that would meet the exacting technical standards of shipmasters and owners.[32]

Fig. 32. Friedrich Richard Petri. **Pioneer Cowpen.** *1853. Watercolor. 4 x 6 3/8 in. (10.2 x 16.2 cm). The Fish Family Trust, Austin, Texas.*

Fig. 33. Friedrich Richard Petri. **Going Visiting.** *1853. Watercolor. 4 x 6 3/8 in. (10.2 x 16.2 cm). The Fish Family Trust, Austin, Texas.*

Fig. 34. Julius Stockfleth. **Galveston Wharf with Sail and Steam Ships.** *c. 1885–86. Watercolor and gouache on paper. 9 x 13 in. (22.9 x 33 cm). The Museum of Fine Arts, Houston, gift of Mr. and Mrs. Kane C. Weiner in honor of Anita K. Weiner at "One Great Night in November, 2003" (2003.707).*

However, Stockfleth also left the only known paintings of the Galveston hurricane of 1900, the greatest natural disaster in the history of Texas. Twelve members of the artist's extended family were among the 6,000 persons killed by the Galveston hurricane; only Stockfleth, his brother, and a sister were spared. All buildings on the beach, which comprised one-fourth of the city's land area, were swept into the Gulf of Mexico; Stockfleth never found any trace of his missing relatives. He attempted to deal with his grief by painting a series of scenes from that weekend of terror. *Tremont Street, Galveston, During Hurricane of September 8, 1900* (fig. 35) depicts a heroic vignette as members of the city's fire department rescue four men from the Tremont Hotel. But even this rescue scene is painted in somber tones and evokes the sentiment of many Galvestonians that the world was ending on that night.[33]

Although he was traumatized for life by the hurricane, Stockfleth remained in Galveston for seven years following the storm. But his paintings did not sell well, despite their low prices; the deteriorated condition of many of these works, due to poor canvas and thin paint, points to the artist's financial hardship. In 1907, finances drove Stockfleth and his widowed sister back to their native village on the North Sea

Fig. 35. Julius Stockfleth. Tremont Street, Galveston, During Hurricane September 8, 1900, 1900. Oil on canvas. 20 x 25 in. (50.8 x 63.5 cm). The William Simpson Family.

island of Föhr. Until his death, he earned a meager living by painting for summer tourists, his neighbors commenting on his deep-seated fear of storms.[34]

The year after much of Galveston was destroyed, the first major oil discovery in Texas, at a salt dome dubbed "Spindletop," hastened tremendously the process of the state's transformation from rural to urban life. Cities such as Dallas and Houston, which depended less on agriculture and more on oil, ultimately supplanted Galveston in importance. The destruction of the cotton port of Galveston and the discovery of oil at Spindletop symbolized a fundamental societal change as Texas moved out of the nineteenth century. The history and way of life in Texas during the preceding era, however, would persist in the paintings of the European immigrants who made Texas their home.

Notes

1 The Jerry Bywaters Collection on Art of the Southwest, housed in the Hamon Arts Library at Southern Methodist University, includes four versions of this drawing executed by the artist, all of them undated. Bywaters' files also contain copies of the Covarrubias illustration. For the most thorough history of the Davis Wildflower Competitions, see William E. Reaves, Jr., *Texas Art and a Wildcatter's Dream: Edgar B. Davis and the San Antonio Art League* (College Station: Texas A&M University Press, 1998).

2 Ray Allen Billington, *Land of Savagery, Land of Promise: The European Image of the American Frontier* (New York: W. W. Norton & Co., 1981), 14–18, 31–34, 196–207, 217.

3 Pauline A. Pinckney, *Painting in Texas: The Nineteenth Century* (Austin: University of Texas Press, 1967), 57, 63.

4 Ibid., 65, 68.

5 McArdle to James T. DeShields, "'Log Cabin' Picture," 2–3, n.d. (c. December 1900), Box 5, File 144. James T. DeShields Collection, Daughters of the Republic of Texas Library at the Alamo, San Antonio. See also McArdle to Governor Lawrence Sullivan Ross, 6 August 1888, quoted in James M. Day, ed., "Texas Letters and Documents," in *Texana* 8:3 (Waco: Texian Press, 1970), 300. In this letter, the artist states that he had begun work on studies of these subjects twenty years earlier.

6 Santa Anna to McArdle, 19 March 1874, translation by Dr. Plutarco Ornelas, Mexican Consul of San Antonio, "McArdle Companion Battle Paintings, Historical Documents, I: *Dawn at the Alamo*," Austin, Texas State Archives, 59.

7 See Taylor to McArdle, 8 March 1886, and "Description of the Painting," in "McArdle Companion Battle Paintings, Historical Documents, II: *The Battle of San Jacinto*," Austin, Texas State Archives, 13.

8 Reuben M. Potter, "The Battle of San Jacinto," *Magazine of American History* 4 (May 1880): 339, 346. Legendary Texas Ranger John S. "Rip" Ford also urged McArdle to feature prominently Captain Antonio Manchaca of Seguin's command (which he did), claiming that it would win friends for the artist in San Antonio, Manchaca's place of residence. See Ford to McArdle, 1 June 1893, "McArdle Companion Battle Paintings, *The Battle of San Jacinto*," 254.

9 Twelve veterans of the battle signed a document attesting to the painting's accuracy during a Texas Veterans Association San Jacinto Day Reunion, 21 April 1891. Two of the more notable signatories were Walter P. Lane and Moses Austin Bryan. See "Endorsement of McArdle's Painting" in "McArdle Companion Battle Paintings, *The Battle of San Jacinto*," 32.

10 McArdle, "Description of the Painting," "McArdle Companion Battle Paintings, *The Battle of San Jacinto*," 13.

11 Ibid. This description also mentions the painting's "wealth of episode" and "that eternal variety and change demanded by a natural presentation."

12 Dorothy Steinbomer Kendall and Carmen Perry, *Gentilz: Artist of the Old Southwest* (Austin: University of Texas Press, 1974), pp. 10, 13. Bobby D. Weaver discusses this survey in *Castro's Colony: Empresario Development in Texas, 1842–1865* (College Station: Texas A&M University Press, 1985), pp. 50–51.

13 See Box A, Folder 33, Gentilz Collection, Daughters of the Republic of Texas Library at the Alamo, San Antonio, hereafter referred to as GC-DRT. Gentilz also noted the total number of figures that he felt should be included in the painting.

14 See Walter Lord, *A Time to Stand* (New York: Harper and Brothers, 1961), 160.

15 See Reuben M. Potter, "The Fall of the Alamo," *Magazine of American History* 2 (January 1878): 11. The first mention of this version of Dickinson's death appeared in Sam Houston's letter of 11 March 1836 to James Fannin in Eugene C. Barker and Amelia W. Williams, eds., *The Writings of Sam Houston, 1813–1836*, 8 vols. (Austin: University of Texas, 1938), 1:362–365. For further discussion of this account, see James A. Shackford, *David Crockett: The Man and the Legend* (Chapel Hill: University of North Carolina Press, 1956), 230; and Lon Tinkle, *13 Days to Glory* (New York: McGraw-Hill, 1958), 144–45. The Arrocha account appears to be excerpted from an interview by Gentilz, Box SM-2, GC-DRT. The author is grateful to Martha Utterback of the Daughters of the Republic of Texas Library for pointing out this interview and for furnishing a translation of Gentilz's French transcription of it.

16 Box A, Folder 1, GC-DRT. See also Susan Prendergast Schoelwer, "The Artist's Alamo," in *Alamo Images: Changing Perceptions of a Texas Experience* (Dallas: DeGolyer Library and Southern Methodist University Press, 1985), p. 436. The first public mention of the Thermopylae parallel appeared in a declaration of 26 March 1836 by the citizens of Nacogdoches commemorating the Alamo defenders. See Schoelwer et al., *Alamo Images*, 5–6.

17 These sketches are found in Box 2, GC-DRT, and a few are described in "Alsatian Artist Pictures Early San Antonio," *San Antonio Light*, 7 October 1945.

18 Quoted in Cecilia Steinfeldt, *Art for History's Sake: The Texas Collection of the Witte Museum* (Austin: Texas State Historical Association, 1993), 152.

19 Ibid., 153.

20 Ibid., 269–271.

21 See James Patrick McGuire, *Iwonski in Texas: Painter and Citizen* (San Antonio: San Antonio Museum Association, 1976), 11, 13, 16–20; and Martha Utterback, *Early Texas Art in the Witte Museum* (San Antonio: Prompt Printers, 1968), 28.

22 See McGuire, *Iwonski in Texas*, 24–25, 76, 78.

23 See ibid., 44; and Paula Mitchell Marks, *Turn Your Eyes Toward Texas: Pioneers Sam and Mary Maverick* (College Station: Texas A&M University Press, 1989), 227–28.

24 See James Patrick McGuire, *Hermann Lungkwitz: Romantic Landscapist on the Texas Frontier* (Austin: University of Texas Press, 1983), 20: and McGuire, *Iwonski in Texas*, 14, 16–18, 20, 25–26, 28–32.

25 See William W. Newcomb, *German Artist on the Texas Frontier: Friedrich Richard Petri* (Austin: University of Texas Press, 1978), 5–8, 13–19. For other discussions of Petri's career, see W. J. Battle, "Art in Texas: An Overview," *Southwest Review* 14 (Autumn 1928): 53; Don Carleton, "Art as Regional History," *Discovery* 6 (Spring 1983): 11; McGuire, *Hermann Lungkwitz*, xi–xvii, 1–5, 9–13; Pinckney, *Painting in Texas*, pp. 74–79; and Lonn Taylor, "Texas Painters of Romantic Frontiers," *Texas Homes* 5 (October 1981): 112.

26 McGuire, *Hermann Lungkwitz*, 55–56.

27 Ibid., 57–59.

28 Newcomb, *German Artist on the Texas Frontier*, 115, 118–20, 138–42.

29 Ibid., 129–130.

30 See ibid., pp. 84, 88 and Taylor, "Texas Painters of Romantic Frontiers," 114, 116.

31 See James Patrick McGuire, Julius Stockfleth: *Gulf Coast Marine and Landscape Painter*, with an Introduction by Eric Steinfeldt (San Antonio: Trinity University Press, and Galveston: Rosenberg Library, 1976), 1–5. These works are part of the slightly fewer than one hundred paintings by Stockfleth having Texas subjects.

32 Quoted in McGuire, *Julius Stockfleth*, 12. For further discussion of shipping along the Texas Gulf Coast during this period, see Steinfeldt, "Introduction," in McGuire, *Julius Stockfleth*, ix–xi.

33 See ibid., 8, 56, 102. For accounts of the Galveston hurricane, see Herbert M. Mason, *Death from the Sea: Our Greatest Natural Disaster, the Galveston Hurricane of 1900* (New York: Dial Press, 1972); David G. McComb, *Galveston: A History* (Austin: University of Texas Press, 1986), 121–49; and John Edward Weems, *A Weekend in September* (New York: Holt, 1957).

34 See McGuire, *Julius Stockfleth*, 10–13.

Fachwerk, Log, and Rock: German Texans' Houses

Kenneth Hafertepe

The many thousands of Germans who immigrated to Texas in the nineteenth century came for many different reasons. Having lived in principalities that were by no means democratic, they sought political freedom. Having lived under an official religion, sometimes Catholic, sometimes Lutheran, they sought the freedom to worship as they chose, or, for a small percentage of settlers, to not worship at all. Having experienced an industrial revolution that was rapidly displacing traditional craftsmen, some sought a place where they could practice the art of cabinetmaking or joinery or stonemasonry. Having come from a land where all the property had been divided centuries earlier, they sought the opportunity to claim their own piece of land.

The transition from German to Texan, and from German to American, was a process that stretched out over several generations. Germans loved much about their old country, even though they cherished the freedom and opportunity of their new home. When the settlers of Fredericksburg celebrated the Fourth of July in 1853, they did so by reading the Declaration of Independence, first in English, then in German. They cherished their native tongue, they loved German food and German beer, and they loved German poetry, songs, and theater. And for most of the nineteenth century, they prayed to God in their native language.

Detail, fig. 3

It would hardly be surprising, then, that Germans brought to Texas their own ideas about how to build their houses, and how to arrange their living spaces. However, those old ways are sometimes hard to define. One of the most important scholars of German-Texan material culture, Terry G. Jordan, observed in *German Seed in Texas Soil* that many German forms like the house-barn, where humans and cattle lived under one roof, were seldom used in Texas. He further argued that German Texans had a distinctive way of building their houses and of farming and ranching. Later in his career, Jordan grew increasingly critical of the notion that Germans had replicated Germany in Texas. His skepticism was fueled by modern-day attempts to make old German-Texan towns more German than they had been in the nineteenth century.[1]

The truth, I think, lies somewhere between Jordan's early and late positions. German Texans did not replicate all of the old ways, but they did retain a great many of them, and German settlers were resistant to Anglo-Texan ways of organizing space. The pioneering generation created a distinctive type of house that was neither purely German nor purely Anglo-Texan. The shift from German to Texan was less a change in attitude than it was a change in generation.

The first generation of German Texans had clear architectural expectations; they wanted a house that was solid and comfortable, and, if they had the means, sociable (fig. 1). Solidity implied that a house was permanent, or at least that it would stand as long as the family might need it. But solidity also spoke to a certain no-nonsense approach: German Texans wanted their houses to be neat, but not necessarily fancy. The comfortable house would be cool in the summer and well heated in the winter, neither too crowded for the family nor with much wasted space, and with sufficient furnishings. The sociable house was one built at a more ambitious scale, for it required a space that would allow for friends and neighbors to join in festivities.

As in many Texas communities, the entire congregation would often pitch in during the construction of a new German-Texan church. The old St. Mary's Church in Fredericksburg (fig. 2), built between 1861 and 1864, has been offered as an example of this. But extensive community involvement should not obscure the fact that such churches—and a great many private houses—were built by trained professionals. The 1921 history of the parish by the Reverend H. Gerlach shows that all of the leading roles were undertaken by trained craftsmen. Father Gerlach listed the workers and what they did; the 1860 U.S. Census reveals that four of these men self-identified their occupation as stonemasons, two others as

Above: Fig. 1. Heinrich and Margarete Bierschwale House, Fredericksburg, Texas, 1872–73.

Left: Fig. 2. St. Mary's Church (the "Marienkirche"), Fredericksburg, 1861–64.

cabinetmakers, and one as a carpenter. Peter Schmidtz and Anton Kraus were the principal stonemasons, Friedrich Gentemann and Johann Kunz made the doors and windows, and Heinrich Cordes took charge of the roof. Only the production of the shingles—and perhaps the nailing of those shingles to the roof—was left to men who identified themselves as farmers. A decade earlier eight men identified themselves as carpenters on the 1850 census, and they were certainly responsible for a great many of the early houses of Fredericksburg.[2]

In addition to examining methods of construction, it is important to think about methods of arranging space. A classic German vernacular plan consists of two rooms, one the *Kuche*, or kitchen, the other a *Stube*, something of a combined parlor and bedroom. In vernacular houses these rooms were side by side, rather than separated by a central passage, as in a typical Anglo-Texan house. If a third space was to be added, it would not be a passage but a *Kammer* or bedchamber separate from the *Stube*. The two-room plan remained popular for decades after Germans arrived in Texas. According to Mathilda Doebbler Gruene, who grew up in and around Fredericksburg, most families had a room for sleeping and a room for cooking and eating.[3]

The earliest German Texans, those who came in the 1830s and 1840s, had the choice to build in one of two ways: log or *Fachwerk*. Log houses, with horizontal logs joined at the corner with notches, had originated in central Europe, and Terry Jordan suggests that eighteenth-century Germans brought the technology to America, where it was rapidly adopted by pioneers everywhere. Ironically, the deforestation of Europe had led to the decline of log construction in Europe, and the new German immigrants had to learn log construction all over again from obliging Anglo-Texans. By contrast, *Fachwerk*, in which a heavy frame is infilled with brick, stone, or even adobe, was a building tradition familiar to many of the immigrants.[4]

An example of this cross-cultural transmission was documented by Herman Seele, a native of Hildesheim. While walking through rural Galveston County in early 1844 he met an Irish-born, Canadian-raised blacksmith, saw his new log house, and admired it greatly: "The simple building, set on high blocks, looked neat and trim; and its plan of construction, two rooms separated by an open central room with a porch in front, made a special impression on me so that I decided to build my own house by this plan some day." In July 1845 Seele and his friend Heinrich Herbst constructed a log house in New Braunfels, "built of cedar logs, with siding and shingles of cypress." It does not seem that they availed themselves of the dogtrot (the open central room or breezeway connecting two parts of a house), at least not right away, as they built one log room in which they lived and a separate log room that served as the kitchen.

The Sophienburg in New Braunfels (fig. 3), the administrative headquarters of Prince Carl of Solms-Braunfels, was documented by a historic photograph taken circa 1878, with a group of original German pioneers arrayed in front. One might hypothesize that this pioneering building had been built by one or more of these early German settlers, but its construction may have been contracted out to nearby Anglo-Americans. Herman Seele recalled that Prince Carl's lodgings were "built by the two Smiths from Seguin." There were several Smiths in the nearby town of Seguin—French, Paris, Charles, and William—all from Virginia and all probably related. French Smith had been one of the founders of Seguin, and in 1838 he had built himself a four-room log house with a dogtrot. At any rate, when the settlement of New Braunfels began, German immigrants were not entirely comfortable using their ancestral building technique.[5]

The windows on the Sophienburg are of two very different types, and in fact speak a different language. At the left is a Germanic double casement window, with four panes in both the left and right casements. The distinctive L-shaped hinges can be found on some of the oldest houses in New Braunfels today, such as the house of Johann Michael Jahn. The window on the right side, however, is an Anglo-Texan

Fig. 4. Goldbeck-Faltin House, Comfort, Texas, 1854, 1856, and after.

Fig. 5. Heinrich and Wilhelmine Cordes House, Fredericksburg, c. 1858.

six-over-six sash window, which did not come into common usage in German communities until the 1850s or, in the Hill Country, after the Civil War.[6]

When Germans did build their own log houses, they did it with the conviction that something worth doing is worth doing right. In log houses of the eastern settlements one finds no little logs or halfhearted dovetailing—the Zimmerscheidt-Leyendecker house near Frelsburg, a community in Fayette County between Austin and Houston, spoke volumes about craftsmanship and permanence. When they expanded the house, however, they chose to fashion their new room with *Fachwerk* construction.[7]

The Texas Hill Country gets far less rainfall than the area around Frelsburg, and as a consequence has fewer and smaller trees. This created a crisis in the mind of German builders who valued solidity and permanence. The solution—as seen in the earliest room of the Goldbeck-Faltin house in Comfort (fig. 4), begun by the brothers Fritz and Theodore Goldbeck in 1854, or in the Heinrich and Wilhelmine Cordes house in Fredericksburg (fig. 5), begun around 1858—was to alternate rows of rocks and logs, with the rocks held in place by solid mortar. Frederick Law Olmsted had already noted that Germans were far more likely than their Anglo-Texan peers to fill in every gap between the logs with chinking, and the German blending of log and mortared rock meant never having to repair the chinking.

When faced with Texas heat, Germans were quick to adopt two features from Anglo-Texans: galleries on one or more sides of their house, and an open passage through the middle, known as a dogtrot in Anglo households and a *Durchgang* in German ones. Dr. Ferdinand Roemer visited Nassau Plantation near Winedale in 1846 and noted that the manor house was "separated into two parts, according to the custom of the country, forming in the center an open, covered passage, which offers the inhabitants a cool, pleasant resort in summer." Dogtrots were used in some log houses and a few *Fachwerk* houses, but galleries would soon be found on German houses across Texas, whether built of log, *Fachwerk*, or rock.[8]

If with the log house Germans were adapting a pioneer housing form common to all Americans, the *Fachwerk* house was much more closely associated with Germans. The frame could be filled with brick, stone or adobe; the result could be left exposed or it could be plastered white, which gave it a more finished look but which also had to be renewed on a regular basis. It could be found in settlements in eastern, central, and west Texas. It could be one, two, or even three rooms, and the two rooms could be side by side or separated by a *Durchgang*.

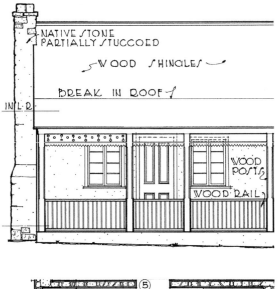

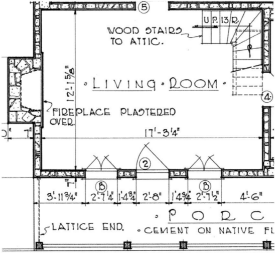

Fig. 6. Adam and Eva Krieger House, Fredericksburg, c. 1847. Original front elevation. Detail from Historic American Buildings Survey drawing by Bartlett Cocke and Anton Heisler, Jr., 1934.

Fig. 7. Adam and Eva Krieger House. Floor plan of original room. Detail from Historic American Buildings Survey drawing by Bartlett Cocke and Anton Heisler, Jr., 1934.

Fig. 8. Adam and Eva Krieger House. Original room looking west.

A good example of the one-room model is the house of Adam and Eva Krieger in Fredericksburg (figs. 6–7). What is now the left front room was the original house. It was infilled with stone and the street facade was quite symmetrical, with the single door flanked by double casement windows. The one room served all purposes, kitchen, parlor, and bedroom, though the front porch also provided livable space (fig. 8). The ceiling beams run from front to back, characteristic of most of these houses. Later rock additions provided a kitchen and two bedrooms, allowing the original room to become a more genteel parlor.[9]

Nearby was the house of Peter and Margarethe Walter (fig. 9). Though small, it was originally divided into two separate rooms. Here the front was asymmetrical from the start, with one door and one window, but both side elevations were perfectly balanced. As with the Krieger house, the frame of the Walter house was infilled with rock, and a later rock addition gave the family a new kitchen. The roof of the Walter house and the other *Fachwerk* houses, which use a common rafter system, are fairly lightly framed, compared to German roofs that might need to support a heavy

Clockwise from top:
Fig. 9. Peter and Margarethe Walter House,
Fredericksburg, c. 1847.

Fig. 10. Johann Jost and Elisabeth Klingelhoefer House,
Fredericksburg, c. 1847. Exterior from the northeast.

Fig. 11. Lyne K. Lewis. **Front Porch, Klingelhoefer**
Home. *Undated. Oil on canvas. 8 x 10 in.*
Private collection.

tile roof. The exposed frameworks of the Krieger and Walter houses make a clear statement about the sturdiness of its construction, reinforced visually and metaphorically by the stone.[10]

The house of Johann Jost Klingelhoefer and his wife, Elisabeth, continued the use of *Fachwerk* and an Anglo front porch, but with an open *Durchgang* (fig. 10). The Klingelhoefer house also had one of the earliest examples of an external staircase. Such staircases seem to have been placed outside because of the German-Texan belief that internal staircases were a waste of valuable space. The spacious porch (fig. 11) and the *Durchgang* were certainly shady and pleasant places to sit; later the *Durchgang* was enclosed by the addition of a rock kitchen and second bedroom. The Klingelhoefer house was unusual for the framing of its ceiling; its large beams run from the walls framing the *Durchgang* to the outer walls. Resting on the large beams are smaller ones that run from front to back. Perhaps this approach was a response to the lack of tall timber in the Hill Country.[11]

The Klingelhoefer house is also the only *Fachwerk* house in Fredericksburg for which the names of the builders can be reasonably hypothesized. The church records of the Vereins Kirche (originally the community church but later Evangelical Lutheran) note that Johann Klingelhoefer's daughter Elizabeth married Herman Hitzfeld in 1851; the marriage is significant because in the 1850 U.S. Census, Hitzfeld identified himself as a carpenter. When Herman and Elizabeth's baby girl Louise was baptized in March 1853, one of the witnesses was Jacob Arhelger, who was also a carpenter. Further, Herman's probate records reveal that in addition to owning some rural acreage and a town lot with buildings and some furniture, $307.25 was owed to Hitzfeld's account by J. J. Klingelhoefer. Perhaps Hitzfeld and Arhelger agreed to build the house if Klingelhoefer paid them over time. Moreover, Jacob Arhelger was born in Rittershausen in Nassau, a mere three miles from Eibelshausen, the birthplace of Klingelhoefer. Even if they somehow had never met, they were familiar with the same German vernacular, both linguistically and architecturally.[12]

The house of Heinrich and Auguste Kammlah represents the largest type of floor plan, with three rooms (figs. 12–13). The center room was smaller and squarish, the outer two larger and rectangular. Presumably the center room was a parlor and the side rooms a kitchen and a bedchamber, but it is unclear which side room was which. One clue is that in addition to an exterior door into the center room, which remains, there was originally an exterior door into the west room. If one takes the west room as a kitchen, it is an example of a kitchen with a direct entry,

Fig. 12. Heinrich and Auguste Kammlah House, Fredericksburg, c. 1847.

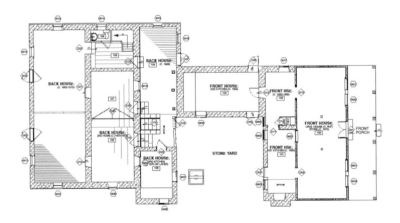

Fig. 13. Heinrich and Auguste Kammlah House. Floor plan. Courtesy Volz and Associates.

Fig. 14. Mount Eliza, the Georg Carl and Elise Willrich House, near Bluff, Texas, 1847. Courtesy of Fayette Heritage Museum and Archives.

or *flurkuchenhaus* plan, which could be found a century earlier in Pennsylvania-German houses. Fairly quickly, however, the Kammlah family added a stone room now known as the first kitchen, which included a small hearth, behind the east front room. The first kitchen was soon superseded in turn by another, larger rock kitchen with a raised hearth in the late 1850s.[13]

In La Grange and other eastern settlements, the preferred material for infill was brick rather than rock. A good surviving example is the 1852 two-room house of John C. Stiehl in La Grange. Stiehl was an attorney and a Fayette County judge. Unlike Germans in the Hill Country, who held onto old-style casement windows, Germans in the eastern settlements quickly adopted double-hung sash windows. This was more typical in Texas, though German Texans preferred nine panes of glass over six rather than the Anglo-Texan norm of six-over-six.[14]

Not all *Fachwerk* houses in the eastern settlements left the framing exposed. Mount Eliza, the house of Georg Carl Willrich and his wife, Elise (fig. 14), had exposed framing on the interior, but clapboards on the exterior that made it hard to distinguish from Anglo-Texan houses. Also Anglo was the use of a central passage, except for three features: it lacked a staircase; both side walls had built-in closets; and at the rear, three steps led down to a very large room that the Willrich family called

Fig. 15. Stephan and Margarethe Klein House, New Braunfels, c. 1846.

Fig. 16. J. L. Forke House, New Braunfels. Side elevation. Photograph for the Historic American Buildings Survey by Richard MacAllister, 1936.

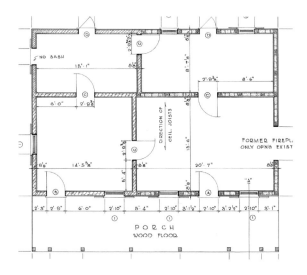

Fig. 17. Goldbeck-Faltin House, Comfort, 1854, 1856, and after. Floor plan. Detail from a Historic American Buildings Survey drawing by Donald Weichlein, 1936.

a *Saal*, not unlike a *salle* in French or a *sala* in Spanish. It was more than a large parlor; it could hold meetings of the Prairie Blume, a local poetry society, or even provide a venue for theatrical groups.[15]

Houses in New Braunfels also used a variety of materials for infill. The house of Stephan and Margarethe Klein (fig. 15), built around 1846, was infilled with rock, while the house of their daughter Anna Maria and her second husband, Johann Michael Jahn, was infilled with brick, and the J. L. Forke house used adobe (fig. 16). Adobe was not something known in the Fatherland, and the German settlers certainly learned it from Hispanic Texans, known as Tejanos, whose population was centered in San Antonio but was also dispersed in surrounding counties. By 1936, enough plaster had fallen off the Forke house to expose the adobe underneath. Such exposure to the elements, however, was a death knell for the infill, and the house was later demolished.[16]

In Comfort, Texas, a community south of Fredericksburg, the Goldbeck-Faltin house started as a one-room log house, but when August and Clara Faltin added on to it they used *Fachwerk* construction (fig. 17, and see fig. 4). The second front room and the room behind it were infilled with rock; when the room on the southwest corner was documented by the Historic American Buildings Survey in 1936, it was infilled with adobe. A more recent owner found that the adobe was impossible to maintain and replaced it with more permanent rock.[17]

Fachwerk houses and log houses flourished in the German settlements only between 1845 and 1860. After the Civil War, most German houses were built of rock, and *Fachwerk* and log were relegated to rural areas and new settlements such as Mason. The rock house certainly possessed the preferred German trait of permanence, but so, too did the *Fachwerk* and log houses, at least the ones that were fortified by brick or stone. It seems quite likely that the end of *Fachwerk* came when stonemasons were painstakingly chipping away at rocks to fit them into the tiny corners of the wooden framework, and realized that it would be easier to skip the framing and just build walls of solid rock.

Two of the earliest rock houses were built in 1850, one in Round Top, the other in Fredericksburg. The house of Conrad and Wilhelmine Schuddemagen in Round Top was built by Wilhelmine's father, the stonemason Carl Sigismund Bauer (fig. 18). The historical marker attached to the house makes the dubious claim that it was "a replica of the family home in Wiesa, Kingdom of Saxony." Actually this is a house that could pass for an Anglo house from the outside, but inside has a very German-Texan arrangement. Bauer and the Schuddemagens certainly got the idea

Fig. 18. Conrad and Wilhelmine Schuddemagen House, Round Top, 1850. Built by Carl Sigismund Bauer. Photograph from Historic American Buildings Survey by Harry L. Starnes, 1936.

Fig. 19. Friedrich and Maria Kiehne House, Fredericksburg, 1850. Photograph from Historic American Buildings Survey by Richard MacAllister, 1936.

for the two-story gallery under an inset porch—that is, the porch does not project forward from the main roof but is fitted underneath it—somewhere on their way from Galveston to Houston to Round Top. Such inset porches, common in Creole houses, abounded in the coastal era. Most of them were one story but some more ambitious examples were two.

The bilateral symmetry of the facade—window, door, window—and the precise centering of the double doors suggested that the house had a central passage, that hallmark of Anglo-Texan interior planning. But these large double doors led directly into the larger of two downstairs rooms, a large squarish sitting room or *Stube*. Again, German Texans seem to have considered a central passage to be a waste of space; instead, the Schuddemagens tucked a staircase at the rear of the smaller room.

The house of Friedrich and Maria Kiehne was the first two-story house in Fredericksburg, and perhaps the first rock house (fig. 19). The limestone was quarried at Cross Mountain on the northwest side of town, a fact noted in the 1896 volume marking the fiftieth anniversary of the founding of the town. Friedrich

Fig. 20. John Peter Tatsch House, Fredericksburg, 1856.

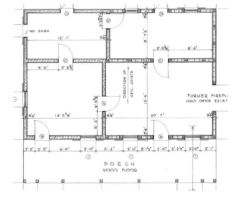

Fig. 21. John Peter Tatsch House. Floor plan.

Kiehne, a hardy blacksmith, was still alive to tell people about it. As with the Schuddemagen house, the Kiehne house had a two-story gallery set beneath the main roof. The lack of a central passage was more obvious, as there was a staircase on the gallery and both front rooms had their own exterior doors. Massive double doors led into the east room, while a more delicate French door opened into the west room. The original windows had four fixed panes of glass at the top and casements beneath. Perhaps the most German thing about the house is the keystone over the east front door. Painted over a plaster base are the names of Friedrich and Maria, complete with her maiden name, and the date of construction. Date stones are often found in Germany and in Pennsylvania German houses, but they are very rare among German Texans.[19]

Interestingly, the wall between the two front rooms is not stone but *Fachwerk*. That is, the framing of the door, complete with a transom-like opening above, is exposed. No documentation links the house to a specific builder, but it should be noted that when the Gillespie County Commissioners decided to build a two-story rock courthouse in 1854, they hired the carpenter Jacob Arhelger rather than any

Fig. 22. John Peter Tatsch House.
South front room.

Fig. 23. Johan Peter Tatsch House.
View of shelf over door between the two
front rooms, and view to built-in shelves
on west wall of north front room.

of the stonemasons working in town. This suggests that he had some experience at constructing two-story rock buildings. Moreover, the interior transom in the Kiehne house was similar to one in the Klingelhoefer house, which Arhelger may have built with Herman Hitzfeld.

The 1856 rock house of John (Johann) Peter Tatsch, a joiner, turner, and cabinetmaker, presents a one-story version of the two-room plan (figs. 20–21). The front door leads into the south room, and the north room originally had a rear door. The squarish south room is larger, and has no fireplace, but does have a flue for a cast-iron stove. The north room has a small fireplace and an internal stair leading to the garret. Though the evidence is not conclusive, it seems that the south room was the *Stube*, using a cast-iron stove for heating, and the north room was the original *Kuche*, or kitchen.[20]

As a skilled woodworker, Tatsch would certainly have crafted his own doors and window frames and probably the stairs. Most striking, however, are the built-in cabinets (figs. 22–23). The cabinet in the north room is really just open shelving, but the cabinet in the south room is smaller and has a paneled door, well suited for Bibles, books, documents, and other valuables. Such cabinets and shelves can be found in *Stuben* in Germany, and in German areas of Pennsylvania. Another telling detail is the shelves which project above the inner door which connects the two rooms and above the north room cabinet.[21]

Like most of the Fredericksburg *Fachwerk* houses, the Tatsch house received a rock addition, a kitchen underneath a shed roof. It is most notable for the massive chimney stack on the north side, which has become a logo of sorts for modern-day tourist Fredericksburg. It is also a huge anomaly, because its modern-day fame obscures the fact that it spawned almost no imitators. Inside, one can see the raised hearth and bake oven. This was one of several raised hearths, most notably in the second kitchen of the Kammlah house, circa 1859, but also in some postwar houses.

Such simple houses are now rare because most were enlarged over time. A remarkably intact, non-enlarged house is the house of Johann Traugott Wandke and his wife, Christiane, in Round Top, built around 1864. The door led into the larger of two rooms, this one heated by a fireplace. The south room, which had an encased stair leading to the loft, had no evident source of heat.[22]

Considerably more ambitious was the house of the stonemason and brewer Heinrich Kreische in the Bluff community, aptly named for its site looking down on the town of La Grange from across the Colorado River (figs. 24–25). In 1856 Kreische and his bride, Josepha, built a rock house with three rooms down and one

Fig. 24. Heinrich and Josepha Kreische House, near La Grange, Texas, 1856 and after.

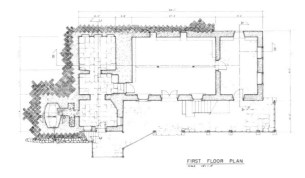

Fig. 25. Heinrich and Josepha Kreische House. First floor plan. Texas Parks and Wildlife.

FIRST FLOOR PLAN

room and a porch above. The three downstairs rooms were roughly equal in size, and all three had stone walls and vaulted ceilings. The northernmost room had no means of heating and would have been a cool storage place for the family's foodstuffs, wine, and beer. The other two rooms served several purposes: kitchen, laundry, and perhaps a downstairs sitting room. Just to the west of the kitchen unit was a large above-ground stone cistern, shaded at the top by a *Fachwerk* room. An external stair led to a covered porch and one large room heated by a corner fireplace, which certainly served as a parlor and bedchamber.[23]

Sometime just before or after the Civil War, Kreische expanded the house dramatically, with a very large dining room downstairs (fig. 26), an equally large parlor above, and two bedrooms. While a parlor (or *Stube*) was common, a dining room was quite rare in German-Texan houses in the antebellum era. Moreover,

Fig. 26. Heinrich and Josepha Kreische House. Ground floor dining room.

this dining room and parlor were so large that they could only have been planned for community events or visits of friends and extended family. On such sociable occasions Kreische was sure to have served the beer that he brewed on the premises, and that he sold under the name "Bluff."

The house of the merchant Wilhelm (William) Neese in Warrenton, between Round Top and La Grange, built sometime between 1854 and 1872, did an even better job of passing for Anglo than the Schuddemagen house. It was two stories, stone, and very symmetrical (figs. 27–28). Unlike the Schuddemagen house, the double doors of the Neese house actually did lead into a central passage linking four rooms, the typical Anglo-Texan plan. However, Neese could not or would not take it all the way, and decided not to put a staircase in the passage. Rather, the stair was tucked in a corner of the right rear room, providing access to the second

Fig. 27. Wilhelm Neese House, Warrenton, Texas, 1854–72.

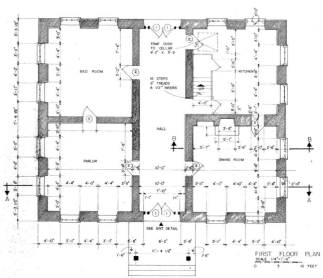

Fig. 28. Wilhelm Neese House, Warrenton. First floor plan. Detail from Historic American Buildings Survey drawing by William Barlow.

Fig. 29. Johann C. and Regina Beckmann House, San Antonio. 1860. J. H. Kampmann, builder. San Antonio Conservation Society.

floor and to a wine cellar in the basement. Two-thirds of the upper floor was given over to a ballroom, a great example of a German Texan wanting to provide for a space for social occasions.[24]

In San Antonio, the house of the blacksmith Johann Conrad Beckmann and his wife, Regina, was built in 1860 by J. H. Kampmann (fig. 29). This austere, almost severe rock house had a flat roof, a classical cornice which ran only across the front facade, and a porch with its roof supported by a pair of stern Doric columns. The windows were six-over-six, more Anglo and modern than the casement windows or nine-over-six windows preferred by many Germans. When the Beckmanns celebrated their golden wedding anniversary in 1891, the San Antonio *Daily Express* noted that "the parlor and hall-way of the residence were a perfect bank of sweet-scented flowers, over sixty bouquets being received." We thus know that the floor plan included a central passage.[25]

Above: Fig. 30. Kammlah House, exterior of new house. Photograph from Historic American Buildings Survey by Richard MacAllister, 1936.

Right: Fig. 31. Kammlah House, parlor of new house.

After the Civil War a new type of German-Texan house emerged in Fredericksburg, the story-and-a-half, two-room rock house. One of the best documented is the house of Heinrich Bierschwale (see fig. 1). Thanks to the meticulous recordkeeping of the owner, we know the cost of the materials, the names of the craftsmen, and what they were paid. Work was begun on the house in June 1872, and it was completed by March 1873, at a cost of $1,200. George Peter was the principal stonemason, Jacob Schneider did most of the carpentry, Heinrich Cordes built the roof, and Engelbert Krauskopf provided the hardware. The craftsmen were paid a total of $613.05, slightly over half of the total cost. The lion's share of Peter's masonry work was done in June, July, and August, after which the other craftsmen really got to work.[26]

Heinrich Bierschwale recorded buying thirteen and a half gallons of whiskey between June 3 and October 14. He bought a gallon every ten days on average at a price of $2 per gallon. The whiskey flowed during the three months of masonry work and the month of roofing. The last gallon was purchased October 14. It may be inferred that the heavy work was finished at that point, and that Jacob Schneider preferred to do his finish carpentry sober.

The Bierschwale house had a large squarish front room that served as a *Stube*, and a kitchen behind it. The *Stube* was heated by a cast-iron stove, as seen from the opening for a flue on the west wall. The stairs to the upper half-story were in the kitchen, tucked against the wall of the *Stube*. This arrangement was seen in several postwar houses, although a few others continued to use external staircases. The Bierschwale kitchen also had a raised cooking hearth in the west wall, opposite the stairs.

The many story-and-a-half houses being built in Fredericksburg encouraged the Kammlah family to expand their house (fig. 30). The new house, completed by 1875, was rock rather than *Fachwerk*, but like their earlier *Fachwerk* house it was comprised of three units: a parlor (fig. 31), a bedroom, and a sort of proto-bathroom. This new unit also included a large cellar under the parlor and bedroom and a loft above it all. With the completion of the new house, the old one was converted into a general store.

The story-and-a-half house also was utilized in the country. On the bluffs above Crabapple Creek north of town, Conrad and Margarethe Welgehausen—both children of Hill Country pioneers—enlarged an original one-room log house with rock rooms to each side (fig. 32). Another range of three rooms was added to the rear at a later date. The original log-and-rock room became the parlor, the room

Fig. 32. Conrad and Margarethe Welgehausen House, near Fredericksburg, center log room c. 1862, rock additions c. 1873 and after.

Fig. 33. Conrad and Margarethe Welgehausen House. View from center room into west room.

to the east a bedchamber, and the room to the west the kitchen (fig. 33). When a new lean-to kitchen was added, the west room became a dining room.[27]

While a few one-story rock houses in Fredericksburg were built with a central passage in the decade after the Civil War, the most monumental central passage house in Gillespie County was the home of Diedrich and Katharina Rode, known as the Rode-Kothe House, in Cherry Spring (fig. 34). This couple acquired land in the northwestern part of the county in 1853, and there they lived in a log-and-rock house for more than twenty-five years. In September 1879, they began work on a large new house, and on June 12, 1880, they moved in. The Rode house was two and a half stories with a very full attic. The two-story front porch contained a staircase from the first floor to the second, and had a cistern attached to the porch at one side, not unlike the arrangement at the Kreische house in Fayette County.[28]

The house had a fully developed central passage plan with four rooms on each floor. The hallway was twenty feet wide, and was used for dining when large groups assembled. The two front rooms were bedrooms; presumably one of these doubled as a parlor in the typical German usage. The northwest room was the kitchen and

Fig. 34. Diedrich and Katherina Rode House (Rode-Kothe House), Cherry Spring. 1879–80.

Fig. 35. Edward and Johanna Steves House, San Antonio, 1876. Designed by Alfred Giles, built by J. H. Kampmann.

the northeast room was Diedrich's shop. Upstairs were two more bedrooms and a large room that could be used for religious services if necessary, as the Rodes were devout Lutherans. The half-story above this was open to the ceiling; it was used to store wool and cotton that Rode would later ship to market. For all its grandeur of scale, the Rode family spent very little ornamenting their house.

Meanwhile, in San Antonio many Germans were leading the development of a residential neighborhood on the south side of town, the King William District. Edward and Johanna Steves turned to a recent arrival in town, the English-trained architect Alfred Giles (fig. 35). Apparently Giles began as the in-house draftsman for J. H. Kampmann, who by 1875 was the dean of San Antonio builders. By the time the Steves house was completed, it was clear that Giles was the architect and superintendent and that Kampmann was relegated to the role of contractor.

Whereas Hill Country rock houses were made of rough-hewn limestone, the Steves house, built 1874–76, had finely crafted and fitted stonework, with round-arched windows and doors. Ornament was concentrated on the front porch, the bracketed cornice, the painted wooden shingles, and the cast-iron crest rail. Inside,

Fig. 36. Edward and Johanna Steves House. Stair hall. San Antonio Conservation Society.

Fig. 37. Edward and Johanna Steves House. Dining room. San Antonio Conservation Society.

Giles, Kampmann, and Mr. and Mrs. Steves not only embraced the Anglo ideal of the central passage, they made it the aesthetic focal point of the interior (fig. 36). The first-floor rooms included a sitting room and dining room (fig. 37) connected by a segmental-arched double door, a parlor, and an office for Mr. Steves. Dining rooms, especially, had been a rarity among German Texans. The Steves house went far beyond the earlier ideal of a sturdy yet cozy rock house into the realm of Victorian elegance.[29]

Fredericksburg and the Hill Country did not fully enter the Victorian era until the late 1880s, when Dr. Albert Keidel and William Bierschwale built their houses, in 1888 and 1889, respectively. Albert was the son of Dr. William Keidel, the earliest physician in Fredericksburg. William was the son of Heinrich Bierschwale, farmer, teacher, and long-time county clerk. Albert followed his father into the medical profession, studying in Germany, while William succeeded his father as county clerk in 1898.[30]

Albert Keidel purchased a story-and-a-half rock house on Main Street in 1881, and seven years later began a dramatic enlargement to a full two stories in an "L" shape, with decorative quoins at all corners and a date stone. Clearly Albert and Mathilde Keidel were aware of the fine homes being built on King William Street in San Antonio, especially those by Alfred Giles. William and Lina Bierschwale went one step further: they hired Giles himself. Giles had already worked in Fredericksburg in 1881, providing the design for the new Gillespie County

Fig. 38. William and Lina Bierschwale House, Fredericksburg, 1889. Designed by Alfred Giles.

Courthouse. The plan and form of the Bierschwale house are strikingly similar to the Keidel house: even the date stone is in exactly the same place (fig. 38).

The distinction of the Bierschwale house was in its finer stone work, which was to be comparable to the officer's quarters at Fort Sam Houston, which were also designed by Giles. Indeed, in his specifications for the Bierschwale house, Giles wrote that "the whole of the Masonry where not otherwise described to be first class rustic rubble work (similar to Officer's Quarters at San Antonio) of rock from the best local quarries well laid in mortar." On the Bierschwale house, Giles used stonework that was rusticated—and rustic—not unlike that of earlier houses, but refined by the carving of the quoins, lintels, and sills. It was, indeed, "first class rustic rubble work."[31]

Most other houses that aspired to mainstream Victorian elegance were one-story versions of the "L"-plan, such as the house of Emil and Emma Beckmann. In 1908 they had set up their household in the old log-and-rock house of Friedrich and Christine Sauer, probably using it pretty much as had the Sauers: a rock kitchen and log parlor in front, with a rock storage room and a bedroom behind. But the young couple dreamed of something different, something more modern, and, around 1915, Emil and Emma built their dream house (fig. 39). It was L-shaped, with a large front porch and a small back porch. Entering from the front porch, one came into a central passage; the parlor was to the right, the back door ahead, and Emma and Emil's bedroom (fig. 40) and the children's room were to

Fig. 39. Emil and Emma Beckman House, Stonewall, Texas. c. 1915. Now the Sauer-Beckmann Living History Farm.

Fig. 40. Emil and Emma Beckman House. Parlor.

the left. The exterior was sheathed in pressed tin, which was designed to resemble stonework. Wallpaper gave the interior of the house a finished look that had been rare in the Hill Country.[32]

Emil and Emma Beckmann clearly did not wish to live in the log houses or even the rock houses of their grandparents or parents. They embraced the ability of modern industry to create the materials of their new home. Apparently the Beckmanns did not dream of having a dining room, though such rooms had become the norm in most Texas houses, or perhaps they had dreamt of it and decided that it was an extravagance. Whatever the case, they had completed the house in which they would live for the rest of their lives.

After a decade or so of experimenting with *Fachwerk* and log, most German Texans settled on rock as their building material of choice. So did many Anglo-Texans, but German Texans insisted on arranging interior spaces their own way, with a parlor and a kitchen, and perhaps some bedrooms above. This way of building persisted into the 1890s, though central passages began to appear in the 1870s and full-blown Victorian houses in the late 1880s. These steps moved Germans away from their ethnic distinctiveness, their German-ness, first toward a distinct German-Texan vernacular, and later toward the American mainstream. This is only to be expected; this is what they came for: to merge into Texas and merge into America. But in the 1920s and 1930s, the solidity, simplicity, and permanence of their old buildings thrilled architects like David R. Williams and O'Neil Ford, who were seeking a new architecture based on the Texas vernacular. Ironically, when German Texans had finally joined mainstream America, mainstream America began to admire the legacy of the pioneering generations of Germans who had gone before them. It is a legacy that we can still admire today.

Notes

1 Terry G. Jordan, "German Houses in Texas," in *Landscape* 14:1 (Autumn 1964): 24–26; Terry G. Jordan, *German Seed in Texas Soil* (Austin: University of Texas Press, 1966), 35–36, 95–96, 165–67; Terry G. Jordan, "German Folk Houses in the Texas Hill Country," in *German Culture in Texas,* eds. Glen E. Lich and Dona B. Reeves (Boston: Twayne, 1980), 103–120.

2 H. Gerlach, *Commemorative Volume for the 75th Year Jubilee of St. Mary's Parish of Fredericksburg,* Texas, trans. Stephen E. Montgomery, Jr. (Fredericksburg, Texas: 1995), 23–31.

3 Mathilda Doebbler Gruen Wagner, *I Think Back: Being the Memoirs of Grandma Gruen, as Told to Her Granddaughter Winifred Cade* (San Antonio, 1937), 4, 11. On different German floor plans and their adaptation to German homes in Pennsylvania, see William Woys Weaver, "The Pennsylvania German House: European Antecedents for New World Forms," *Winterthur Portfolio* 21:4 (Winter 1986): 243–64; Charles Bergengren, "Pennsylvania German House Forms," in *Guidebook for the Vernacular Architecture Forum Annual Conference: Architecture and Landscape of the Pennsylvania Germans, May 12–16, 2004, Harrisburg, Pennsylvania* (n.p.: Vernacular Architecture Forum, 2004), 23–46; and Cynthia G. Falk, *Architecture and Artifacts of the Pennsylvania Germans: Constructing Identity in Early America* (University Park: Pennsylvania State University Press, 2008), 19–29, 40–41, and 65–79.

4 Terry G. Jordan, *Texas Log Buildings, A Folk Architecture* (Austin: University of Texas Press, 1978), 21–27.

5 Herman Seele, *The Cypress and Other Writings of a German Pioneer in Texas*, trans. Edward C. Breitenkamp (Austin: University of Texas Press, 1979), 24–25, 69. On the Smiths of Seguin, see E. John Gesick, Jr., *Under the Live Oak Tree: A History of Seguin* (Seguin, Texas: Seguin State Bank and Trust Company, 1988), 47, 53, 57, 59, 60, 61; and the 1850 United States Census for Guadalupe County, households 43, 149, 150, and 183. The log rooms of the French Smith house were incorporated in a larger house for George Hollamon. Mrs. Edwin Harris, ed., *Historic Homes: The Charm of Seguin* (Seguin, Texas: Seguin Conservation Society, 1986), 18.

6 Oscar Haas, *History of New Braunfels and Comal County, Texas, 1844–1946* (Austin: privately printed, 1983), 29; Seele, *The Cypress*, 24. The 1881 bird's-eye view shows that the rear of the building had two small windows and a centered inset gallery.

7 This house was placed on the National Register of Historic Places in 1979, but two years later it was burned to the ground by an arsonist. Historic American Buildings Survey, TX 313; Jordan, *Texas Log Buildings*, 17; Cecilia Steinfeldt, *Art for History's Sake: The Texas Collection of the Witte Museum Association* (Austin: Texas State Historical Association for the San Antonio Museum Association, 1993), 132–33; Lonn Taylor, "Sweet Potatoes and Cicero: Furniture and Furniture-Making in the German Settlements of Texas," in *American Material Culture and the Texas Experience: The David B. Warren Symposium*, vol. 1 (Houston: The Museum of Fine Arts, Houston, 2009), 94, 96.

8 Ferdinand Roemer, *Texas: With Particular Reference to German Immigration and the Physical Appearance of the Country*, trans. Oswald Mueller (San Antonio: Standard Printing Company, 1935), 163.

9 Elise Kowert, *Old Homes and Buildings of Fredericksburg* (Fredericksburg: Fredericksburg Publishing Co., 1977), 150; Historic American Buildings Survey, Texas 33-A-8.

10 Ibid., 92–94.

11 Ibid., 38–39; Gillespie County Historical Society, *Pioneers in God's Hills* (Austin: Von Boeckmann-Jones, 1960), 1:94–95.

12 *Pioneers in God's Hills*, 1:94–95, 229, 273; Ella A. Gold, trans., *Kirchen-Buch*, 102, 16, 142, 144, 104; 1850 United States Census, in *Pioneers in God's Hills*, 2:213.

13 Elise Kowert, *Historic Homes in and around Fredericksburg*, (Fredericksburg Texas: Fredericksburg Publishing, 1980) 6–8; *Pioneers in God's Hills*, 2:243; Volz & Associates, *Kammlah House Historic Structures Report* (Austin: n.p., April 2009).

14 Historic American Buildings Survey, Texas 3121; Taylor, "Sweet Potatoes and Cicero," 92, 96.

15 Mrs. George Willrich, wife of the grandson of George and Eliza, cited in Leonie Rummel Wade and Houston Wade, *An Early History of Fayette County* (La Grange, Texas: printed by the *La Grange Journal*, 1936), 235.

16 Historic American Buildings Survey, Texas 33-A-10 (Klein) and TX-373 (Forke); Donald L. Stover, *Tischlermeister Jahn* (San Antonio: San Antonio Museum Association, 1978), 11.

17 Historic American Buildings Survey, TX-376; conversation with Mr. August Faltin III, February 2003.

18 Historic American Buildings Survey, Tex-3123; Fayette County History Book Committee, *Fayette County, Texas Heritage*, vol. 2 (Curtis Media, 1996), F65, F985, F 986.

19 Kowert, *Old Homes and Buildings*, 41–43; *Pioneers in God's Hills*, 1:92–93, 276; *Pioneers in God's Hills*, 2:216; *Kirchen-Buch*, 5, 7, 12; C. L. Wisseman, trans., *Fredericksburg, Texas, The First Fifty Years: A Translation of Penniger's 50th Anniversary Festival Edition* (Fredericksburg, Texas: Fredericksburg Publishing Company, 1971), 34. On datestones as a German ethnic feature, see Falk, *Architecture and Artifacts of the Pennsylvania Germans*, 183–84.

20 Kowert, *Old Homes and Buildings*, 5–6; *Pioneers in God's Hills* 1:213–15; *Pioneers in God's Hills* 2:246; Historic American Buildings Survey, 33-A-12.

21 For a Pennsylvania example, see the shelf over the internal door of the Heinrich Zeller house, west of Newmanstown, Pennsylvania.

22 Historic American Buildings Survey TX-3188.

23 Todd McMakin and James E. Corbin, comps., *An Archeological Assessment of Kreische Brewery State Historic Site, Fayette County, Texas* (Austin: Texas Parks and Wildlife, 2001); and John J. Leffler, *The Kreisches and Their World: The Kreische Family, the Bluff Community and Life on "Kreische's Bluff,"* 1840–1960 (Austin: Texas Parks and Wildlife, 2008).

24 Historic American Buildings Survey, TX-3520.

25 Frederick Charles Chabot, *With the Makers of San Antonio* (San Antonio: Artes Gráficas, 1937), 375–77; "Anniversary," *San Antonio Daily Express*, November 8, 1891; Beckmann obituary, *San Antonio Daily Express*, April 13, 1907; Sanborn Fire Insurance Map for San Antonio, July 1885, sheet 4.

26 *Pioneers in God's Hills* 1:13; *Pioneers in God's Hills* 2:190 (1860 census); Kowert, *Old Homes and Buildings*, 140–42. In 2010 the account was in the possession of Mrs. Lindy Bierschwale Haley.

27 Kowert, *Historic Homes*, 63.

28 Historic American Buildings Survey, TX-378; Kowert, *Historic Homes*, 170–79. One of the Rode grandchildren, Mrs. E. C. Fiedler, shared Rode's meticulous diaries with Kowert.

29 Mary Carolyn Hollers George, *Alfred Giles: An English Architect in Texas and Mexico* (San Antonio: Trinity University Press, 1972), 48–50; see also Mary Carolyn Hollers George, *The Architectural Legacy of Alfred Giles: Selected Restorations* (San Antonio: Trinity University Press, 2006), 26, 38–39, 44; Historic American Buildings Survey, TEX-3150; *A Guide to San Antonio Architecture*, 73; and Cynthia A. Brandimarte, *Inside Texas: Culture, Identity, and Houses*, 1878–1920 (Fort Worth: Texas Christian University Press, 1991), 78–82.

30 Kowert, *Old Homes and Buildings*, 104–06, 116–18.

31 George, *Alfred Giles*, 39.

32 Marian L. Martinello with Ophelia Nielsen Weinheimer, *The Search for Emma's Story: A Model for Humanities Detective Work* (Fort Worth: Texas Christian University Press, 1987), 15–37, 44, 155–91.

Scarlett Doesn't Live Here Anymore: Tara, *Gone with the Wind*, and the Southern Landscape Tradition

Maurie D. McInnis

If you were to ask an audience today to identify the most famous southern plantation, many would probably name Tara (fig. 1), the fictitious plantation in the 1936 novel and 1939 film *Gone With the Wind*. Nothing has had a greater impact on creating a shared memory of the Old South as a romantic place of harmony, grace, and refinement than has the movie version of Margaret Mitchell's novel. It remains the most watched movie of all time. Long before video and DVDs, the movie was only occasionally shown at movie theaters. I'll never forget the first time I saw it. It was at the historic Tennessee Theater in Knoxville, which was then a bit shabby, but it was a really grand old theater complete with its Wurlitzer organ. I was only a young girl then, but I remember being swept away by the epic quality of the movie. I also remember when it was shown for the first time on television in 1977, just weeks after the unexpected success of the television miniseries *Roots*. What contrasting perspectives of the Old South those two productions presented. *Roots* flipped *Gone with the Wind* inside out.[1]

Fig. 1. Scene from **Gone with the Wind**. *M-G-M/ Turner Entertainment Co.*

Out of the contradictory perspectives of *Roots* and *Gone with the Wind* grew my own academic interest in history that attempts to deal with the inconsistencies and complexities of the American past. I find that novels and movies often possess an unshakeable hold on my students' ideas about the past. Almost none of them have seen *Roots*, but many of them have seen *Gone with the Wind*. Even though they were born after 1990 and have never known life without cell phones, DVD players, and computers, nearly every one of my female students has watched it and even most of my male students have seen at least part of it. Many students rank it among their favorite movies (although I think it is mainly Clark Gable that holds their attention). The movie (if adjusted for inflation) is still the highest grossing movie of all times. The novel, too, was and continues to be extraordinarily popular. By the time the movie premiered in 1939, more than two million copies had been sold. Today, it has been translated into sixteen languages and, more than seventy years later, it still sells more than a quarter of a million copies a year.

Although the movie is seventy years old, it has spawned and continues to support an amazing industry. You can get almost anything with Scarlett and Rhett on it: dolls, cookie jars, plates, models of houses, among numerous other items. The proliferation of imagery from the movie has come to dominate the way that many imagine the South in the nineteenth century. While it is ostensibly a book and movie about the period just before, during, and after the Civil War, it is in so many ways more about the 1930s Depression than it was about the earlier era. Audiences found the story of prosperity and triumph over war, poverty, and hardship reassuring.

While it was a story particularly attuned to a world on the brink of war—when the movie premiered in December 1939, Hitler had already invaded Poland, and in the next few months he would invade Denmark, Norway, and France—the stories from the movie did much to shape a national historical narrative that presented the antebellum period as a golden age when prosperity prevailed, racial hierarchy meant harmony, perseverance paid off, and the past gave meaning to the present. This essay will consider the vision of the antebellum past set forth by Mitchell and by the movie's producer David O. Selznick in relationship to that depicted by artists in the nineteenth century. In so doing, we will see the ways in which *Gone with the Wind* was (and was not) inspired by the past and how it has forever changed the way we remember the past.[2]

Certainly one of the most enduring images from the movie is Tara. As Scarlett ran past the white peacocks roaming the front lawn to greet her father, she established a visual icon of the graceful South before the Civil War. Selznick's movie version, however, had little to do with the prewar South about which Mitchell had written. The author described Tara as a house "built according to no architectural plan whatever, with extra rooms added where and when it seemed convenient, but . . . it had gained a charm that made up for its lack of design."[3] In a letter written after the book was published but before the movie was made, Mitchell said that people asked her why she hadn't made Tara "a Greek Revival House." That was the image that audiences expected, one fueled by Hollywood movies such as *So Red the Rose* (1936), which featured a house fronted by a monumental portico framed in the opening shot by live oak trees dripping with Spanish moss. In contrast to the vision Hollywood typically provided of the Old South, Mitchell replied that she "had to ride Clayton County pretty thoroughly before I found even one white columned house in which to put the Wilkes family."[4] She presented the Wilkes family of Twelve Oaks as a Virginia family of old money. The O'Haras, by contrast, were intended to be first-generation planters. She was adamant that Tara was not a grand home.

Mitchell's Tara, however, would not do for the big screen. Selznick instructed his artistic team to devise a grander Tara, and for Selznick the grandeur of the Old South was symbolized by a house with a large portico of monumental columns. Mitchell hated the movie rendition of her Tara, commenting, "I get sicker and sicker of the damned columns that people wish to put on every southern house."[5] Whereas Selznick's various advisors were telling him that no place in Clayton County, Georgia, would have looked like the Tara he devised, Selznick demanded that moviegoers needed to see the Tara that they imagined, not the one Mitchell described nor the one that might have existed. He knew that in the movie version, viewers would imagine that Tara was "just like the mansion my grandpappy had that Sherman burned."[6] Even though Tara was much grander than what Mitchell had described, Selznick thought that he hadn't been grand enough in creating Tara. He wrote to the art director, Lyle Wheeler, "I am sure that you both share my regret that we didn't go further on the size and beauty on the interior of Tara."[7]

After years of being critical of Selznick's fanciful rendering of the Old South, I have come to realize that he did not make up Tara completely out of the blue. Selznick's Tara was intimately tied to a historical artistic trajectory that began with the painting of plantation house portraits in the early nineteenth century. This tradition continued after the war, as the way that artists depicted the past influenced how that past was remembered.

Landscape painting in the South had long been identified with individual plantation properties. Wealth and status were closely tied to the land. In emulation of English practice, the earliest landscapes in the southern American colonies were called "overmantels." These were paintings that, as their name suggests, hung over the mantel such as the one at George Washington's Mount Vernon (fig. 2). This was a tradition adapted directly from England, and sometimes, as is the case at Mount Vernon, the mantel itself was copied directly from designs printed in English architectural pattern books. Early overmantels were generic, picturesque landscapes, often of indeterminate places, based on English precedent.

With time, such works came to be celebrations of individual properties such as *Rose Hill*, an overmantel painting of a South Carolina Low Country rice plantation (fig. 3). *Rose Hill* embodies a well-established visual formula. While the house sits at the apex, the foreground is filled with a sweep of manicured lawn. Surrounding the house are outbuildings typically found on a working plantation. On the left hand side, a large threshing barn and a rice-winnowing house sit idle while large

Fig. 3. Unknown artist. **Rose Hill**. *c. 1820. Oil on canvas,*
36 1/2 x 51 1/2 in. (90.2 x 130.8 cm). Charleston Museum, Charleston, S.C.

stacks of hay suggest the fecundity of the land. These buildings thus refer to the
source of wealth, but labor and agricultural production are not shown. Horses and
sheep graze in the right foreground, and the only hint of the hundreds of slaves
who lived and worked on the property is the figure of a man crossing the large
expanse of lawn with a fanner basket on his head.

Such plantation scenes often include figures at leisure. In the case of *Rose Hill*,
there are several figures in the left foreground engaged in shooting birds.[8] The
house at Rose Hill was far more modest than the imagined Tara, yet images such as
these formed an important precedent for the way in which Tara was depicted. In
the early renderings created for Selznick, artists followed a similar formula (fig. 4).
Tara sits at the apex of the compostion, nestled in trees. The outbuildings that
stretch to the right of the house are visually lost in the dominant image of the main
house with its monumental white-columned portico.

Overmantel paintings such as the one of Rose Hill grew out of a landscape
painting tradition in the South Carolina Low Country that began as early as the

Above: Fig. 4. **Gone with the Wind, exterior of Tara.**
*David O. Selznick Archive, Harry Ransom Humanities
Research Center, the University of Texas at Austin.*

Below: Fig. 5. Thomas Coram. **The Seat of T. Radcliffe,
Esquire.** *c. 1800. Oil on paper, 11 3/8 x 9 1/4 in.
(28.9 x 23.5 cm). Gibbes Museum of Art/Carolina Art
Association, Charleston, S.C.*

1790s with the English-born artist Thomas Coram. He was a self-taught engraver and painter and, as such, he learned about painting from books. There he encountered the picturesque style of landscape from English authors such as the Reverend William Gilpin. Coram then applied the lessons about compositional formulas to depict the South Carolina plantation landscape. That proved to be a challenge given that the aesthetic formula usually began with mountainous terrain or ruins framed by a vista. Coram adapted the picturesque formula to South Carolina's landscape by creating vistas, framing views with trees, and making use of the Low Country's abundant rivers, streams, and marshes.

Coram captured the immensity of a planter's holdings by painting multiple views, each guided by the doctrines of the picturesque and only sometimes including either buildings or people. There are two surviving sets of views. The set he made of Almondbury plantation owned by Thomas and Lucretia Radcliffe was comprised of seven paintings (fig. 5).[9] All are still in their original eglomise frames (black and gold reverse painting on glass), and they spell out clearly the point of such images, that is, a record of the ownership of vast amounts of land. Two of the frames read only "T. Radcliffe Esq.," while four read "the seat of T. Radcliffe, Esq." These images spoke to possession; they celebrated the source of wealth with multiple views of the rice fields and other vistas that suggest the immensity of the Radcliffes' holdings. These static views portray the planter's dominion over the landscape and the lives who cultivated the land, and they fix a visual vocabulary of the pastoral ideal as embodied in the southern plantation landscape. The seven images of their plantation property show multiple views of their land, rice fields, and plantation house. Not only did the Radcliffes possess extensive agricultural holdings, but they also built one of the most elaborate homes in the city. The probate inventory taken at the time of Lucretia's death documents that these seven paintings hung in the vestibule of their Charleston home. There, these views of the plantation property would have served as an evocative reminder of the source of their wealth and their status as planters.

The most famous of Coram's works today is one of the seven images he made of Mulberry Plantation (fig. 6). It is unique in its depiction of a row of slave quarters in addition to the mansion house. While the mansion house at Mulberry survives, the slave quarters do not. The representation of these quarters is of particular historical interest because they appear to be earthfast structures—supported on posts sunk in the ground, rather than by a foundation—that may represent an African building practice that would later be replaced by European-derived frame-

*Fig. 6. Thomas Coram. **View of Mulberry, House and Street**. c. 1800. Oil on paper, 4 1/8 x 6 5/8 in. (10.5 x 16.8 cm). Gibbes Museum of Art/Carolina Art Association, Charleston, S.C.*

and-brick structures. The image is also unique because it depicts some of the slaves who labored in the rice fields. There are at least four slaves who have hoes, which they would have used in the rice fields, carried over their shoulders. In this view, the slaves are very small figures, each composed of little more than a few strokes of the paintbrush. Not individuals, they are for the artist merely supporting actors in the larger story of the extraordinary wealth generated by the labor of hundreds of thousands of slaves in the rice fields of South Carolina and Georgia. Like most plantation scenes, the mansion house still emerges as the most important pictorial element in the landscape and the focal point of the composition.

Thomas Coram was not the only artist painting southern landscapes at the beginning of the nineteenth century. In Baltimore, Francis Guy was active painting a similar series of views of Maryland plantations. Both Guy and Coram, who were working in the first decade of the nineteenth century, were painting landscapes before the start of the so-called Hudson River School. In the traditional narrative of the history of American art, Thomas Cole is usually credited as the founder of the American landscape tradition and of the Hudson River School, but it is important to note that Guy and Coran were working almost two decades earlier.

Fig. 7. Francis Guy. **Perry Hall from the Northwest.** *c. 1805. Oil on canvas, 21 13/16 x 30 in. (55.4 x 76.2 cm). Maryland Historical Society, Baltimore, Md.*

Guy's numerous views of Maryland estates and other sites in and around Baltimore are prized for their meticulous renditions.[10] Larger than the views rendered by Coram, those by Guy generally provided a panoramic, sweeping view of the property with a meticulous recording of the architectural details of the mansion house. Many of them also contained numerous small figures. In *Perry Hall from the Northwest* (fig. 7), the planter and his family are depicted strolling the estate. One of the early designs for Selznick's rendering of Tara, featuring a mansion on the hill with a manicured lawn with Scarlett and peacocks in the foreground, borrows heavily from this earlier landscape tradition.

The tradition of painting plantation house portraits continued throughout the antebellum period. Typically, these paintings were commissioned by private owners to represent their personal property. Yet the southern landscape also had a public dimension. The German-born and -trained Edward Beyer traveled in Virginia in the 1850s, primarily in the Shenandoah Valley, creating multiple views of towns, spas, and interesting geological sites. Many of these views he published as lithographs in a book titled *Album of Virginia*.[11] The artist, who had worked previously as a painter of large panorama paintings, depicted the Valley's small market towns

Fig. 8. Currier and Ives. **The Home of Washington, Mt. Vernon, Va.** *1856–72. Hand-colored lithograph, 12.4 x 16 in. (31.4 x 41 cm). Courtesy of the Library of Congress, Prints and Photographs Division, Washington, D.C.*

and spas nestled in the foothills of Virginia's mountains. These meticulously rendered images shared an interest in the details and accuracy of the view.

While most of his views were of towns, he also painted some works for individual owners and of individual plantations. Unlike the earlier paintings by Guy and Coram, in *Bellevue, The Lewis Homestead, Salem, Virginia,* Beyer devotes much of the canvas to the sweep of the valley and the Blue Ridge beyond. In this image, the house is not the dominant visual element. Nestled in the middle ground, only its white color makes it conspicuous. Unusually for antebellum painting, Beyer has depicted slaves working in the foreground. They are working to harvest the abundant hay, and their small forms mimic and are almost indistinguishable from the haystacks they are creating.[12] Everything about the image speaks to the agricultural bounty of the Shenandoah Valley as Virginia's population spread westward.

Beyer's *Album of Virginia* grew out of a long-standing tradition of painting the properties of famous men. The most famous plantation of all was George Washington's Mount Vernon. Images of Mount Vernon were popular during Washington's lifetime and became only more so after his death. As Washington's popularity continued to increase in the nineteenth century, it was the mansion house at his Mount Vernon plantation that for many Americans came to embody the spirit of the man. Visiting the plantation and Washington's burial site became something of a pilgrimage. Dozens of images of the mansion house were produced, in paintings, in books, in prints, and on all sorts of objects like clocks and dinnerware.

The most common view, such as the one published by Currier and Ives, was the one that featured the river side of the mansion house with its piazza stretching across the front, set high on the bank above the Potomac River (fig. 8). Looking up at the house from below, with figures leisurely strolling across the piazza and lawn, helped to solidify an image of the southern plantation as a place of leisurely refinement and natural grace. Mount Vernon's popularity was and continues to be such that there are architectural replicas of Mount Vernon throughout the American landscape. The familiar piazza with its square columns has been used as inspiration for houses, banks, hotels, and a wide range of commercial structures.

As the most replicated southern plantation, it should not be surprising that it influenced the artistic direction of *Gone with the Wind*. The plantation homes that had been painted before the war were the most elite properties of the South. In these images, grand mansion houses usually with columned porticoes were set among perfectly organized and manicured landscaped settings. They generally suggested a life of leisure lived gracefully, with little or no reference to the labor that generated that wealth nor the dirt, disease, and difficulties that really characterized nineteenth-century life. As Selznick set his designers on bringing *Gone with the Wind* to the screen, the appearance of Tara was of primary concern. Designers submitted more than twenty designs that were rejected by the producer (fig. 9).[13] In many of the early designs for Tara, the house more closely resembled early twentieth-century Colonial Revival designs, including those available from Sears (fig. 10), than they did any plantation home that could be found in the antebellum South. Selznick wanted something grander.

But the Tara of the book was not grand. The author later recounted that "in the pages of unwritten history, no fiercer fight was ever fought than the one centering around the columns on the motion picture 'Tara.'" Mitchell's friends, Susan Myrick and Wilbur Katz, Georgians who were hired by the film to help with accents and historical details, tried to keep columns off Tara entirely, but they "managed a compromise by having the pillars square," which Mitchell thought was at least closer to what Upcountry Georgia houses had, if they had columns at all.[14] It was also a form familiar in the minds of all Americans. Although it was not a copy of Mount

*Fig. 9. **Gone with the Wind, Early Rendering of Tara**. David O. Selznick Archive, Harry Ransom Humanities Research Center, the University of Texas at Austin.*

Vernon, the form certainly evoked the familiar structure. In the 1930s, Americans everywhere had been inundated with images of Washington and Mount Vernon as the nation celebrated the bicentennial of his birth in 1932. The resulting Tara would have been a comforting, if inaccurate, evocation.

Mount Vernon had long carried symbolic meaning. Whereas by the 1930s Washington and Mount Vernon symbolized an earlier golden age seemingly devoid of strife, a nation triumphant and prosperous, it had not always been so. In the nineteenth century, the representation of Mount Vernon was employed as part of the period's political and cultural debates. In the 1850s, a series of events and legislative initiatives greatly increased sectional tensions, particularly those regarding slavery. In that atmosphere it is perhaps not surprising that the figure of Washington was used by different sides of the political tensions. Washington could be used as both a pro-Union and a pro-Southern symbol. In the latter guise he was often shown as a planter on his Mount Vernon estate. In these images, such as the widely distributed print produced by Nathaniel Currier of the firm Currier and Ives, Washington's presence as a benevolent planter bolstered the pro-slavery forces who spoke of the

Fig. 10. "The Jefferson," Sears Homes of Today. 1932. Sears catalogue.

institution's civilizing effects (fig. 11). In the image, Washington is not the "Father of Our Country"; he is not the nation's first president; he is instead the nation's best-known slave owner.[15] He is shown on his horse talking with slaves who labor in the wheat fields. The mansion house at Mount Vernon is prominently featured and the abundant wheat in the foreground suggests the fecundity of the property and, by extension, the bounty of southern agriculture.

When Beyer published his *Album of Virginia* in 1858, he also leaned on the popularity of Mount Vernon. He featured that house and Thomas Jefferson's Monticello on his title page, even though neither was illustrated within (fig. 12). He surrounded those images with twirling vines to suggest, as the wheat does in the Currier and Ives image, the bounty of Virginia's land. By the 1850s, however, Virginia's agriculture was not bounteous in the tidewater sections of the state, including the areas where Mount Vernon was situated. Perhaps without meaning to, Beyer alludes to the division between Virginia's past and future as he placed industry and the railroad in the other cartouches on the title page.[16]

Fig. 11. Currier and Ives. **Washington at Mount Vernon, 1797.** *c. 1852.*
Hand-colored lithograph, 8 7/8 x 12 3/8 in. (31.4 x 41 cm). Courtesy of
the Library of Congress, Prints and Photographs Division, Washington, D.C.

Like Beyer, who saw Mount Vernon as a symbol of Virginia's past, a number of
artists found different symbolic meaning in Mount Vernon in the 1850s. Whereas
Mount Vernon has long been represented as a bounteous estate, the reality was that
by 1858 the property had fallen into a state of disrepair (fig. 13). The current state
of the plantation left visitors worried for its future. Under the leadership of Pamela
Ann Cunningham, the Mount Vernon Ladies' Association eventually purchased the
property in 1858 from Washington's great-nephew John Augustine Washington III,
who no longer found the plantation financially remunerative. While many artists
continued to represent the property as the productive plantation they imagined in
Washington's day, others were intrigued by the estate's decay.

Eastman Johnson visited the estate in 1857, and the images he created
eschewed the usually reverential atmosphere that most adopted in their images of
Mount Vernon. Instead, Johnson depicted the Mount Vernon that he encountered
in 1857, dilapidated and in a state of decay. Additionally, Johnson represented the
estate not from the perspective of the white visitor, but instead from the perspective
of the slaves who continued to live and work at Mount Vernon. Rather than focus-

Fig. 12. Edward Beyer. **Album of Virginia**. *1858. Bound lithograph.*
Special Collections, University of Virginia Library, Charlottesville.

ing on the mansion house, in his *Kitchen at Mount Vernon* (fig. 14) he took viewers inside, where a young slave mother sits with her children. The darkened and gloomy painting depicts a building in disrepair. Plaster has fallen off the walls and the building is largely unfurnished and unadorned.[17] Johnson's paintings express a lament—a lament for the decay of Mount Vernon, for the passing of an earlier golden age, and for the current state of southern society based on slave labor.

That sense of decay and of loss had already permeated southern landscape depictions before the Civil War, but the sweeping destruction of the war meant that such imagery became considerably more widespread. Some artists played directly off the earlier imagery, such as Edward Lamson Henry, whose *The Old Westover House* (fig. 15) appears at first to be another southern plantation landscape. Lamson, who was born in Charleston, South Carolina, but later moved to New York, served as a clerk on a Union transport ship, and while in Virginia, he made these sketches at Westover.

Upon first glance, this painting, exhibited in New York only a few years after the war, looks much like a plantation portrait. The surprise comes, however, when

*Fig. 13. Photograph of the east facade of the Mount Vernon Mansion,
c. 1858. Mount Vernon Ladies' Association.*

the viewer realizes that it has been turned inside out and upside down. Union
troops are bivouacked on the front lawn. Next to the tents is a pile of broken furniture, presumably removed from the house and destroyed. Soldiers can be seen not
only at the doorway, but also on top of the house and in many of the windows.
The right flanker to the house is burned out, but, importantly, the house is still
standing. Ultimately, however, it is an ambiguous image. It is not at all clear
whether Henry's painting documents the fall of the South or its continuance.

Loss and destruction in the wake of the war became an important theme for
southern artists. One of the most poignant renderings of this theme is by George
David Coulon. A French-born artist trained in New Orleans, he was best known
for his Louisiana landscapes. The image of the ruins of De la Ronde Plantation,
Versailles, in St. Bernard Parish, Louisiana, captures the spirit of loss that was pervasive throughout the South following the war (fig. 16). Painted about two decades
after the end of the war, an image such as this was a painful reminder of what was
lost. In many ways, the image harkens back to the earlier tradition of plantation
portraits, yet this time, instead of a manicured lawn, there is unruly, overgrown grass;
instead of patrons at leisure, there is emptiness; instead of a grand house, there is

Fig. 14. Eastman Johnson. **Kitchen at Mount Vernon.** *1857.*
Oil on canvas, 14 x 21 in. (35.6 x 53.3 cm). The Hevrdejs Collection, Houston.

merely a ruined shell. The yearning for a bygone era is palpable.

These images of ruin and destruction obviously played a big role in the imagination of Southerners about the past. It became a big part of the memory of the southern landscape. I grew up being constantly told, such-and-such isn't here anymore "because Sherman burned it." While there is some truth to that, there is also a great degree of exaggeration. According to all the "Sherman burned it" taglines I've heard, that man was everywhere—and for decades, too. Things that were burned long after the war are often blamed on him as well. The makers of *Gone with the Wind* knew this. And they decided to play upon that sense of loss and to make the Old South grand enough to lament its passing.

Whereas Tara was clearly an exaggeration, the fictive neighboring mansion at Twelve Oaks was almost ludicrous (fig. 17). Nowhere in the South was there a library as grand as this. The scale and opulence of the interiors could only be found in royal palaces in Europe. Mitchell commented that "many of us were hard put not to burst into laughter at the sight of 'Twelve Oaks.' We agreed afterwards that the only comparison we could bring to mind was with the State Capitol at Montgomery, Alabama."[18] On the movie set, Tara was merely a shell with no rooms

Fig. 15. Edward Lamson Henry. **The Old Westover House.** *1869. Oil on paperboard, 11 1/4 x 14 5/8 in. (7 x 37.1 cm). Corcoran Gallery of Art, Washington, D.C., gift of the American Art Association.*

inside, but Twelve Oaks was too grand to even build and was only a painted backdrop. The sweeping staircase at Twelve Oaks, which was built in a studio, is certainly seared into every moviegoer's mind—grander than grand, it became the staircase that every young girl imagined herself swooshing down to meet a young man as handsome as Clark Gable (fig. 18).

Mitchell remained disconcerted about the opulence of Twelve Oaks. She wrote, "I have been embarrassed on many occasions by finding myself included among writers who pictured the South as a land of white columned mansions whose wealthy owners had thousands of slaves and drank thousands of mint juleps. I have been surprised, too, for North Georgia certainly was no such country—if it ever existed anywhere—and I took great pains to describe North Georgia as it was. But people believe what they like to believe and the mythical Old South has too strong a hold on their imaginations to be altered by the mere reading of a 1,037 page book."[19] That grandeur was vital to creating the painful sense of loss that is central to the story. Thanks to movie magic, Twelve Oaks became real in the minds of moviegoers, and when the camera showed Scarlett standing at the bottom of that staircase where, as a young woman, untarnished by war, blood, fear, and hunger, she had

Fig. 16. George David Coulon. **Ruins of a Louisiana Plantation.** *c. 1885.*
Oil on canvas, 25 x 30 in. (63.5 x 76.2 cm). Collection Stephen Reily, Louisville, Ky.

first met Rhett Butler, audiences everywhere were ready to believe the myth. And then, when Scarlett returns at the end of the war and stands at the base of that same staircase with the ruins of Twelve Oaks around her, audiences were even more willing to curse the destructiveness of war and to lament the loss of the Old South (fig. 19).

There was another strain of southern landscape painting that gained popularity in the postwar years. William Aiken Walker, an artist born in Charleston, had a very successful career after the war marketing an image of the prewar South that recreated an imagined place of orderly and harmonious racial relations. Walker's painting *A Cotton Plantation on the Mississippi* was published by Currier and Ives (fig. 20). Many of his most important patrons were northern cotton factors who still profited from the crop that had led many southerners to believe that the North would never fight in this war. The prints enjoyed a widespread popularity. Cotton's central place in the national economy and its international importance led Senator James Henry Hammond of South Carolina to make a famous boast in 1858: "Without firing a gun, without drawing a sword, should they make war on us, we could bring the whole world to our feet. . . . What would happen if no cotton was

Fig. 17. **Gone with the Wind, Hall at Twelve Oaks.** *David O. Selznick Archive, Harry Ransom Humanities Research Center, the University of Texas at Austin.*

Fig. 18. **Gone with the Wind, Staircase at Twelve Oaks.** *David O. Selznick Archive, Harry Ransom Humanities Research Center, the University of Texas at Austin.*

furnished for three years? . . . England would topple headlong and carry the whole civilized world with her save the South. No, you dare not to make war on cotton. No power on the earth dares to make war upon it. Cotton is King."[20]

Interestingly, while cotton was the main export for the United States in the decades leading up to the Civil War, it is not until the postbellum period that it becomes the central image of the plantation South. In images such as those by Walker, cotton plantations and African Americans picking cotton become the central defining symbol of the plantation South. Nowhere is modernity evident, and the human footprint is typically quite small. Whether we are talking about landscapes in the North or the South, in the postwar period there was a longing for quiet. There was nostalgia for a simpler life that is clearly anti-modern, anti-urban, and anti-industrialization, and the South was seen as a place that embodied that.[21]

The near invisibility of slave labor in the images of southern plantations was another pictorial element that the artists perpetuated in their designs for the movie. Agriculture and slave labor play very little part in the telling of *Gone with the Wind*, in part because agriculture had failed just about everyone in the 1930s, and in part because it is a movie mostly told from the perspective of whites. In the trailer for the movie, slavery is hinted at in an image of a cotton press and an image of a slave cabin, but in the final cut of the movie, slavery, and especially labor, are largely absent.

The ways in which the film designers conceived of including slavery mimicked the approach of the earliest artists, such as Coram. In a design for an opening scene of the movie, the slaves were merely anonymous figures seen from a distance working in the field (fig. 21). They were much like the small figures carrying hoes in Coram's view of Mulberry (see fig. 6). Much like the figures in Beyer's painting, the slaves blend into the landscape. They serve merely as visual props to the central story of prosperity embodied in Tara. They were meant to be suggestive of the past and an important set element, much like the grand houses and elaborate costumes.

Two of the overarching themes of the movie are that war is futile and men cannot be relied upon. It is important to note that Margaret Mitchell wrote this in the wake of World War I, where her fiancé had been killed. The postwar good years for Scarlett were not in the cotton fields of the South but were instead bound up in Atlanta and business, and yet at the end, it was to Tara and to the past that her mind returned. The movie was released in 1939, at a time that the entire nation was beset with an economic crisis, and when the South and agriculture had been hit particularly hard—and it struck a reassuring chord. The ideas that after hardship

Fig. 19. **Gone with the Wind, Staircase at Twelve Oaks after the Fire.** *David O. Selznick Archive, Harry Ransom Humanities Research Center, the University of Texas at Austin.*

Fig. 20. Currier and Ives, after William Aiken Walker. **A Cotton Plantation on the Mississippi.** *1884. Lithograph, 21 x 30 in. (53.3 x 76.2 cm). Courtesy of the Library of Congress, Prints and Photographs Division, Washington, D.C.*

life would rebound, that in the past there was hope for the future, were immensely attractive messages. The movie appealed to the South for obvious reasons, but it also appealed to the industrial North, where waves of immigration and massive growth and dislocation in urban settings had left many feeling unconnected and wary of modernization. The images of the past they turned to were ones that elided the past's true complexities. They were ones that spoke of economic prosperity, racial harmony, gracious living, and the importance of continuity and tradition.

This was, of course, not the reality of the South in the twentieth century, but it is a way of thinking about the South that continues. The opening lines of the movie, which were not written by Mitchell, were quite accurate—not the ones that put forth the South as the "land of Cavaliers," but the ones that described it as a "dream remembered." The "dream" of the Old South put forward by the filmmakers was one informed by nineteenth-century images, including landscape paintings, that were in themselves ideals. As historians and art historians have studied the nineteenth-century past, we know the many ways in which *Gone with the Wind* is

*Fig. 21. **Gone with the Wind, Fields—Opening Shots**. David O. Selznick Archive, Harry Ransom Humanities Research Center, the University of Texas at Austin.*

inaccurate. Many have written eloquently on racial and gender complexities that are omitted from the film.

In the same decade, there were other artists who represented a very different past, for example, the author William Faulkner and the painter Jacob Lawrence. The past put forward in *Gone with the Wind* was instead a romanticized, premodern South, one built on patriarchy, familial relationships, and ties to the land. It idealized an already idealized image of the South. As Scarlett's world falls down around her, and Rhett utters his famous retort—"Frankly, my dear, I don't give a damn"— her answer is to return to the land. She will go home to Tara because, as her father once told her, land is the only thing that matters, the only thing that endures. For the *Gone with the Wind* audience in 1939, the idea that "tomorrow is another day" was comforting. A decade into the Depression, with another war looming in Europe, the ambiguous ending left room for hope and a new future, but the source of strength for the future was one that looked to the past. So while we know that Scarlett doesn't live here, and that she never lived here, examining her vision of the nineteenth century can tell us a lot about her moment in the 1930s. And while historians have done much to help all of us to remember a history of the nineteenth-century South where Scarlett doesn't live, it is remarkable how strongly Scarlett's South endures.

Ultimately, even Mitchell understood the power of Selznick's vision of the prewar South. In a letter to historian Virginius Dabney, Mitchell jokingly said, "I believe that we Southerners could write the truth about the antebellum South, its few slaveholders, its yeomen farmers, its rambling, comfortable houses just fifty years away from log cabins, until Gabriel blows his trump—and everyone would go on believing in the Hollywood version. The sad part is that many Southerners believe this myth even more ardently than Northerners. A number of years ago some of us organized a club, The Association of Southerners Whose Grandpappies Did Not Live in Houses With White Columns."[22] For most Americans, however, it is Scarlett's South of white columns and Southern belles that endures.

Notes

1 As a compelling historical sidenote, *Roots* was broadcast not long after the television premiere of *Gone with the Wind*. The final episode of *Roots* became the third most watched television event in history and (if you remove sporting events) the television broadcast premiere of *Gone with the Wind* was the fourth most watched event. Such rankings proliferate on the internet and all agree that *Roots* had the third highest viewership as measured by percentage of households. The farewell episode of *M*A*S*H* was first, and the "who shot J.R." episode of *Dallas* was second. *Gone with the Wind* was fourth (and fifth) if you do not count sporting events, and eighth and ninth if you do.

2 The bibliography on *Gone with the Wind*, both book and movie, is extensive. I have only cited from the sources most directly related to this article.

3 Margaret Mitchell, *Gone with the Wind* (New York: Macmillan, 1936), 57.

4 Margaret Mitchell to Stephen Vincent Benet, July 9, 1936, *Margaret Mitchell's "Gone with the Wind" Letters*, 1936–1949, edited by Richard Harwell (New York: Macmillan, 1976), 34–36.

5 Margaret Mitchell to Wilbur G. Kurtz, March 11, 1939, Margaret Mitchell Family Papers, Hargrett Rare Book and Manuscript Library, University of Georgia, Athens, quoted in Alexis L. Boylan, "From Gilded Age to *Gone with the Wind*," in *Landscape of Slavery: The Plantation in American Art*, edited by Angela D. Mack and Stephen G. Hoffius (Columbia: University of South Carolina Press, 2008), 134.

6 "*Gone with the Wind*" *Letters*, 271–72, quoted in Edward D. C. Campbell, Jr., "The Old South as National Epic," in *Gone with the Wind as Book and Film*, ed. Richard Harwell (Columbia: University of South Carolina Press, 1983), 178.

7 Selznick to Wheeler, quoted in Aljean Harmetz, *On the Road to Tara: The Making of Gone with the Wind* (New York: Harry N. Abrams, 1996), 63.

8 See also Angela D. Mack, "Introduction," in *Landscape of Slavery*, 3–4.

9 See also Roberta Sokolitz, "Picturing the Plantation," and Maurie D. McInnis, "The Most Famous Plantation of All," in *Landscape of Slavery*, 30–39, 89–90.

10 See Sokolitz, "Picturing the Plantation," in *Landscape of Slavery*, 41–43 and John Michael Vlach, *The Planter's Prospect: Privilege and Slavery in Plantation Paintings* (Chapel Hill: University of North Carolina Press, 2002), 49–65.

11 William M. S. Rasmussen and Robert S. Tilton, *Old Virginia: The Pursuit of a Pastoral Ideal* (Charlottesville, Va.: Howell Press, 2003), 64–65.

12 Ibid., 107.

13 Harmetz, *On the Road to Tara*, 62–64.

14 Margaret Mitchell to Virginius Dabney, July 23, 1942, in *"Gone with the Wind" Letters*, 358.

15 McInnis, "The Most Famous Plantation of All," *Landscape of Slavery*, 89.

16 Rasmussen and Tilton, *Old Virginia*, 64–65.

17 For a more extensive discussion, see McInnis, "The Most Famous Plantation of All," in *Landscape of Slavery*, 105–109.

18 Margaret Mitchell to Virginius Dabney, July 23, 1942, in *"Gone with the Wind" Letters*, 357–59.

19 Ibid., 359.

20 James Henry Hammond, "Speech of Hon. James H. Hammond, of South Carolina, On the Admission of Kansas, Under the Lecompton Constitution: Delivered in the Senate of the United States, March 4, 1858" (Washington, D.C., 1858).

21 See Nina Silber, *The Romance of Reunion: Northerners and the South*, 1865–1900 (Chapel Hill: University of North Carolina Press, 1993).

22 Margaret Mitchell to Virginius Dabney, 23 July, 1942, *"Gone with the Wind" Letters*, 357–59.

As God Has Made It:
Painting the American Southwest before 1900

Michael R. Grauer

"God never made an ugly landscape." —John Muir, *Atlantic Monthly* (January 1869)

Anyone who has seen a sunrise in the Texas Panhandle and a painting by Frank Reaugh of the same subject would have to acknowledge the painter's clear talent (see detail opposite and fig. 11), even while willingly crediting that higher, "greatest painter of all." Indeed, the perception of natural beauty in America—from Ralph Waldo Emerson's God-filled nature to the work of Thomas Moran and Frederic Edwin Church (fig. 1)—underscores the important connections between late nineteenth-century artists at work in the dangerous Southwest and those early nineteenth-century painters who found prestige and recognition in the East.

In the spirit of Miss Ima Hogg, who strove to overcome Texas's isolationism by bringing early Americana to Bayou Bend, it might be helpful to put late-nineteenth-century Southwestern art into the broader context of nineteenth-century American painting. We will consider the geographically, but not intellectually, distant Transcendentalist movement that first rose out of 1830s New England, set the

Detail, fig. 11

groundwork for the Hudson River School, and then—alongside the writings of American naturalists John Muir and John Burroughs—illuminated the landscapes of Yosemite and the American Southwest.

Nineteenth-Century Foundations: Transcendentalism and the Natural Sublime

The idea of the hand of God in American nature structures nineteenth-century attitudes about the American landscape from Emerson to John Ruskin, and from Church to Moran. In his groundbreaking 1836 essay *Nature*, Emerson (1803–1882) expresses his conviction that God permeates all of creation. This founding text of Transcendentalism famously celebrates that loss of self that takes place as the believing seer submits to God and Nature. Emerson finds himself "glad to the brink of fear" as he witnesses divinity in nature. In the "plantations of God," he finds a "perennial festival," and his famous account is pointed ever upwards towards the heavens, as he returns to "reason and faith": "Standing on the bare ground,—my head bathed by the blithe air, and uplifted into infinite space,—all mean egotism vanishes. I become a transparent eye-ball; I am nothing; I see all; the currents of the Universal Being circulate through me; I am part or particle of God."[1] Significantly, transcendence and vision are linked. Indeed, this metaphorical blending of sight, truth, and God are central to understanding nineteenth-century attitudes toward nature.

At the same time, science and exploration sought a clearer view of American nature particularly in the West, as both famous and now-forgotten expeditions set out into unknown territories. In 1819–20, U. S. Army Major Stephen H. Long's southwestern expedition took his party from Iowa up the Platte River, across today's Nebraska to the front range of the Rocky Mountains, then south in search of the Red River, planning to follow it back to civilization at Fort Smith, Arkansas Territory. However, crossing what is now the Texas Panhandle, Long mistook the Canadian River for the Red; heading east, party members suffered from thirst and starvation, eventually eating their horses before arriving in Fort Smith. While Long's report revealed mistaken geographies, his portrait of the Plains in words— that "Great American Desert"—remained in the American lexicon, and even postponed settlement for fifty years.

Accompanying Long were Samuel Seymour (1775–1823), who painted vistas along the route, and Titian Ramsey Peale (1799–1885), who focused on the Plains' flora and fauna. For many, including the late-nineteenth-century naturalist John

Fig. 1. Frederic Edwin Church. **Twilight in the Wilderness.** 1860. Oil on canvas, 40 x 64 in.
(101.6 x 162.6 cm). The Cleveland Museum of Art, Mr. and Mrs. William H. Marlatt Fund (1965.233).

Burroughs (1837–1921), such a gathering of information and views further chronicled
the omnipotence of God and proved the Romantic joining of seer, God, and nature.
The details of the landscape were powerful, and it mattered how we described it.
Writing in the context of the battle between science and religion, Burroughs offered
the following counter: If we call nature's power "God," "it smells of creeds and
systems, of superstition, intolerance, [and] persecution; but when we call it Nature,
it smells of spring and summer, of green fields and blooming groves, of birds and
flowers and sky and stars." Burroughs shifting of vocabulary matters here because
it accomplishes an extension of God's hand in nature, even if by a changed name.
Even disasters like "tornadoes and earthquakes, . . . disease and death," Burroughs
writes, make Nature "more real to us" and still prompt us—albeit in the wake of
science—"to conceive of God in terms of universal Nature," a God of nature "in
whom we really live and move and have our being, with whom our relation is as
intimate and constant as that of the babe in its mother's womb, or the apple upon
the bough. This is the God that science and reason reveal to us—the God we touch
with our hands, see with our eyes, hear with our ears, and from whom there is no
escape."[2] Nature may have been chronicled, measured, and made known by science,

but for Burroughs, who inherits Emerson's Transcendental vision, God's hand is still at work. Moreover, in science as well as art, the merging of the conceptions of the Beautiful and the Sublime—celebrated by Burroughs and articulated earlier by Edmund Burke (1729–1797), William Gilpin (1724–1804), and John Ruskin (1819–1900)—provided Americans with the means to "see" nature and divine power through the lens of art.

Burke, reinvigorating these key aesthetic terms as he laid a foundation for nineteenth-century Romanticism, suggested that the aesthetic concept of the Sublime in nature—alpine mountains, craggy cliffs, broken trees, and crashing waterfalls—inspires terror, wildness of spirit, and overwhelming power. In landscapes by the Italian painter Salvator Rosa (1615–1673), for instance, nature cannot offer man a home—it is far too powerful, unpredictable, and threatening. By contrast, the concept of the Beautiful connoted a curving softness of form: rolling hills, gentle streams, and trees in full bloom—landscapes where mankind could reside peacefully and in harmony with Nature,[3] as in the classical-inspired paintings of Claude Gelée (called Le Lorrain) (1600–1682). By locating aesthetic response in emotions rather than reason, the Burkean Sublime opened the way to early Romantic interpretations of landscape. With the harmonious landscapes of Thomas Gainsborough receding into the past, the nineteenth century courted the power of nature, heralded imagination and emotion over the intellect, and foreshadowed yet another renaming of God in natural creation: the Romantic Sublime, which would inspire poetry and art for much of the coming century.

In step with his British contemporaries during the heart of the Romantic period, William Wordsworth (1770–1850) acknowledged and praised the presence of God in nature—even if indirectly. While God is never called by name when Wordsworth looks on nature, he nonetheless feels a "presence that disturbs [him] with the joy / Of elevated thoughts." Like Emerson some three decades later, standing on the bare ground and feeling his thoughts ascend through divine nature, Wordsworth describes "elevated thoughts" and a "sense sublime":

> Of something far more deeply interfused,
> Whose dwelling is the light of setting suns,
> And the round ocean and the living air,
> And the blue sky, and in the mind of man;
> A motion and a spirit, that impels
> All thinking things, all objects of all thought,
> And rolls through all things.[4]

Fig. 2. Thomas Cole. **Indian Pass**. 1847. Oil on canvas, 40 1/16 x 29 3/4 x 1 7/16 in. (101.8 x 75.6 x 3.6 cm). The Museum of Fine Arts, Houston, museum purchase with funds provided by the Agnes Cullen Arnold Endowment Fund (95.138).

Fig. 3. Jasper Francis Cropsey. **Autumn on Greenwood Lake.** *1861. Oil on canvas, 24 1/4 x 38 3/8 in. (61.6 x 97.5 cm). The Museum of Fine Arts, Houston, gift of Wells Fargo (2006.577).*

New Western Wilderness: The Hudson River School and Its Legacy

Forging an American tradition, Thomas Cole (1801–1948) practiced and advanced landscape painting in America. Considered the father of the "Hudson River School," Cole ventured into upstate New York from his native Britain in the 1820s, searching for a "wild America" to paint. In particular, he sought the Sublime in nature, often placing a device such as a storm-blasted tree strategically in the foreground of his paintings, as in *Indian Pass* (fig. 2). These dark and foreboding elements highlight the "wildness and overwhelming power" of nature and foreshadow the later locus of that wild Sublime in America's unexplored West.[5] Yearning for official confirmation, Cole sought to bolster his standing through a Grand Tour in 1829. However, William Cullen Bryant, wanting to ensure that his great friend would not forget his American experience, admonished Cole to "keep that earlier, wilder image bright" in his consciousness as he gazed upon the Italian *campagna* and other European landmarks. In other words, Bryant begged Cole to retain the wilder and Sublime parts of American nature.[6]

Not long after, Asher B. Durand (1796–1888)—more a follower of Cole than a true student—began in the late 1830s to combine a Colesian reconciliation of the real and the ideal with pure landscape without figures, ushering in a relatively new convention of figureless landscapes. Durand remained influenced by Ruskin's insistence on some measure of carefully observed detail in painting. Consequently, Durand's landscapes evolved from fairly typical, generalized Claudean scenes to compositions including foregrounds painted in near-scientific detail. Nevertheless, his tour de force painting, *Kindred Spirits* (1849)—an homage to Cole—celebrates the strong connections between the landscape painter and the nature writer at the midpoint of the nineteenth century by including the poet and journalist Bryant.[7]

As the Hudson River School reached its apex in the 1850s, science continued to be part of the artistic conversation in the United States, particularly through images produced from government expeditions to the Southwest. For example, the earliest known images (now lost) of Palo Duro Canyon in the Texas Panhandle are from military expeditions. In March 1852, Mexican War veteran and trailblazer Captain Randolph Marcy headed an expedition across the Great Plains, seeking the source of the Red River; his charge was to "collect and report everything that may be useful or interesting." Marcy's party crossed a thousand miles of previously undocumented lands in Texas and present-day Oklahoma. As part of another Western expedition, Heinrich Mollhausen (1825–1905) joined Lieutenant Amiel Weeks Whipple's Pacific Railroad survey of the 35th parallel as "topographer or draughtsman." In 1853–54, the party traveled from Fort Smith, Arkansas, to Pueblo de los Angeles in California. Mollhausen's drawings and watercolors were reproduced as chromolithographs in Whipple's report, including several images of the Texas Panhandle. In spite of Mollhausen's devotion to science, his detailed images are laced with Romantic depictions of how he thought or hoped the landscape should and would look.[8]

Meanwhile, Cole's only true student, Frederic Edwin Church (1826–1900), initially followed in his mentor's footsteps, but soon took his own direction, searching for the Sublime in nature. Even though Church chose not the American West but instead South America, Alaska, New England, and Niagara Falls as his playing field, his approach to these images laid foundations for Western wilderness painting. Some scholars believe his choice of South America was heavily influenced by the naturalist work of Alexander von Humboldt. That is, by adding science to mix in the tension between the real and the ideal, Church took Durand's devotion to Ruskinian specific-nature studies to a new level. Moreover, as in Romantic poetry, Church's particular interest seemed to be the cyclical parts of nature, especially those characteristics involving water. Like his contemporary John Muir (1838–1914), who sought the "words of God" in high Sierra "rocks and waters," Church seemed to infuse his images of water with divine power. After Transcendentalism and the Hudson River School, God was sought less in chapels and altars and more in the grand creation of nature itself: "God does not appear, and flow out, only from narrow chinks and round bored wells here and there in favored races and places, but He flows in grand undivided currents, shoreless and boundless over creeds and forms and all kinds of civilizations and peoples and beasts, saturating all and fountainizing all."[9]

As the Hudson River School gained prominence in the American art world, other painters emerged. Jasper Francis Cropsey (1823–1900) (fig. 3), Robert Scott Duncanson (1817–1872) (fig. 4), and Ralph Albert Blakelock (1847–1919) all practiced this aesthetic. The Hudson River School formula usually included laterally framing trees, a mediating figure in the middle ground, alternating patches of light and dark from foreground to background, and a body of water that meandered into the background, guiding the viewer's eye to the light, openness, and God-filled beauty in the distance.

Though his German training might place him outside the mainstream of the Hudson River School, Albert Bierstadt (1830–1902) nonetheless remains central to the movement. First venturing West in 1859, Bierstadt returned again in 1863, but not before exhibiting his first masterpiece, *The Rocky Mountains, Lander's Peak* (The Metropolitan Museum of Art, New York). Bierstadt's presentation of this 1863 canvas closely parallels Church's staging of his *Heart of the Andes* a few years earlier. A description of Church's unveiling can just as easily describe Bierstadt's: The painting's frame had drawn curtains fitted to it, creating the illusion of a view out a window. Church even brought South American plants to further set off the painting. Equipped with opera glasses, audience members sat on benches to view the piece as Church darkened the room and spotlighted the landscape painting. Capitalizing on the current craze for panoramas, and long before "performance art" became a common phrase, Church and Bierstadt compressed panoramic views onto a single piece of canvas in what our own age might call an "interactive" showing.

While Church was focused on locales beyond the American West, Bierstadt took to Yosemite, which he approached as a "natural cathedral." Upon arrival in those granite spires, Bierstadt announced that he was "in the new Garden of Eden,"[10] and he echoed, in his paintings, the inspired accounts of John Muir:

*Fig. 4. Robert S. Duncanson. A View of Asheville, North Carolina.
1850. Oil on academy board, 13 x 18 13/16 in. (33.0 x 47.8 cm).
The Museum of Fine Arts, Houston, gift of the Susan Vaughan
Foundation in memory of Susan Clayton McAshan (2001.85).*

No Sierra landscape that I have seen holds anything truly dead
or dull, or any trace of what in manufactories is called rubbish or
waste; everything is perfectly clean and pure and full of divine
lessons. This quick, inevitable interest attaching to everything
seems marvelous until the hand of God becomes visible; then it
seems reasonable that what interests Him may well interest us.
When we try to pick out anything by itself, we find it hitched
to everything else in the universe.[11]

Artists continued to take risky, adventurous trips to the West after the Civil War.
Worthington Whittredge (1820–1910), Sanford Robinson Gifford (1823–1880),
and John Frederick Kensett (1816–1872)—normally associated with the Hudson
River School (fig. 5)—traveled to Denver, Colorado, by train in 1870.[12] Whittredge
had already visited the West, accompanying the Pope Expedition to the Southwest in
1866. From Fort Leavenworth, Kansas, the party traveled up the Platte River to

*Fig. 5. John Frederick Kensett. **Distant View of the Mansfield Mountain, Vermont**. 1849. Oil on canvas, 48 x 39 5/8 in. (121.9 x 100.6 cm). The Museum of Fine Arts, Houston, museum purchase with funds provided by the Hogg Brothers Collection, gift of Miss Ima Hogg, by exchange; the Houston Friends of Art and Mrs. William Stamps Farish, by exchange; and the General Accessions Fund (76.200).*

Denver, then down the Rockies to Albuquerque, New Mexico Territory, and back to Fort Riley, Kansas. Whittredge painted the earliest known view of Santa Fe during this trip and crossed the Llano Estacado, or Staked Plains, putting his party in the Texas Panhandle. The three artists painted mainly north and east of Denver, migrating up into Wyoming Territory. Later in the summer, Gifford joined the United States Geological Survey into the Rockies under Dr. Ferdinand V. Hayden, accompanied by photographer William Henry Jackson. Jackson photographed Gifford making one of the most famous field sketches in art history of the American West (fig. 6), showing the geological connections between the northern and southern parts of the West.

In 1871, Thomas Moran (1837–1926) joined Hayden and Jackson in the U.S. Geological Survey of Yellowstone, then called Coulter's Hell. Moran's resulting watercolors and Jackson's photographs were circulated through the halls of Congress and, within seven months of this trip, Yellowstone became the first national park. Congress later purchased his monumental canvas *Grand Canyon of the Yellowstone* to hang in the Senate Lobby of the United States Capitol. Two years later, Congress purchased Moran's *Chasm of the Colorado*, a result of his 1873 trip to the Grand Canyon with John Wesley Powell.

Moran, like Church—and to a lesser extent Bierstadt—highlighted the cyclical images of nature as an expression of the hand of God, particularly in water imagery. His travels took him all over the West and into Mexico. In 1875, Moran completed the third of his great Western landscapes, *Mountain of the Holy Cross*, a view of a famous Colorado peak where a cross was formed in snow (fig. 7). Moran echoed Cole and Gilpin in his attempt to paint an "impression" of the scene rather than a view in the topographical tradition, and, in this case, he entirely invented the foreground waterfall. His friend Jackson also captured the Mountain of the Holy Cross in a photograph, before a landslide erased the crevasses that allowed the cross to appear. The Transcendentalists' location of God in nature, and particularly in the American West, found no greater confirmation than this natural phenomenon.

Emerson had lain the foundations for these late nineteenth-century painters, calling for that still undeveloped voice of the American wilderness and pleading for a talent that would describe native beauty and would—with him—locate the divine hand in American nature. He lamented that he still "look[ed] in vain" for that "genius in America" who would have a "tyrannous eye" and who would know "the value of our incomparable materials": "Our logrolling, our stumps and their politics, our fisheries, our Negroes, and Indians, our boasts, and our repudiations, the wraths of rogues, and the pusillanimity of honest men, the northern trade, the southern

Above: Fig. 6. Sanford Robinson Gifford.
Valley of the Chugwater, Wyoming Territory.
1870. Oil on canvas, 7 3/4 x 12 7/8 in.
(19.7 x 32.7 cm). Amon Carter Museum of
American Art, Fort Worth, Texas (1970.67).

Left: Fig. 7. Thomas Moran. **Mountain**
of the Holy Cross. *1875. Oil on canvas,*
82 1/8 x 64 1/4 in. (208.6 x 163.2 cm).
Museum of the American West, Autry
National Center, Los Angeles, donated by
Mr. and Mrs. Gene Autry.

Opposite: Fig. 8. Vincent Colyer. **On the Big**
Canadian River (On the Big Canadian,
Indian Territory). *1869. Watercolor on*
paper mounted on paper, 7 1/2 x 13 1/4 in.
(19 x 33.6 cm). Panhandle-Plains Historical
Museum, Canyon, Texas, Friends of
Southwestern Art Purchase.

planting, the western clearing, Oregon, and Texas, are yet unsung. Yet America is a poem in our eyes; its ample geography dazzles the imaginations."[13]

During the last third of the nineteenth century, despite advances by Cole, Moran, and even Bierstadt in Yosemite, Texas and most of the greater Southwest largely eluded the painter's brush. Moreover, while much of southeastern Texas was settled, its western hills, plains, and canyons remained unexpressed. These lands—with their arid expanses, sparse settlements, and ever-present dangers from Indian tribes—remained, as Emerson might say, "unsung" in American art and letters. Artists were simply lucky to make it across the Southern Plains and into the Southwest without being raided or killed. Comanches and Kiowas—and later Cheyennes and Arapahoes—ruled the Southern Plains from the early nineteenth century until 1875. Indeed, John C. Fremont's ill-fated 1848–49 expedition into southern Colorado led to the killing of artist Richard Kern by Utes.

The territory controlled by the Comanches—the Comancheria—included most of Texas and Indian Territory, running west to the Rio Grande in New Mexico Territory and extending north into southwestern Kansas and southeastern Colorado. Euro-American settlers in southeast Texas and other parts of the Comancheria lived in great fear of the next Indian attack. European migrations in the 1850s, however, increased the Euro-American presence in Texas. U.S. Army officer Seth Eastman, stationed at San Antonio in the 1849, created paintings of those lands. Elsewhere in Texas, painters, including Theodore Gentilz, Richard Petri, and Carl G. von Iwonski, focused almost exclusively on genre painting.[14] Petri's brother-in-law, Hermann

*Fig. 9. John Clifford Cowles. J A Panorama (**Palo Duro Canyon**). 1887. Oil on canvas, 38 x 58 in. (96.5 x 147.3 cm). Panhandle-Plains Historical Museum, Canyon, Texas, gift of Amarillo Federated Women's Club, Inc.*

Lungkwitz, added to Texas landscape painting with his views of the Pedernales River. Lungkwitz's work from the 1860s and 1870s could hang alongside the best of the Hudson River School painters, yet he had no connection to the British landscape tradition from which these eastern artists descended.

In spring 1869, landscape painter Vincent Colyer (1825–1888) traveled across Indian Territory from Fort Gibson (near today's Tulsa) on assignment from the newly created Board of Indian Commissioners. Colyer's 1869 assignment was to ascertain conditions among Indians on the Southern Plains and in New Mexico Territory.[15] Among American artists, Colyer was in a unique position to advise the Board of Indian Commissioners, as he had served on the U.S. Christian Commission during the Civil War. A Quaker from Bloomingdale, New York, he became a serious artist and was elected as associate of the National Academy of Design, where he had studied. He exhibited large-scale paintings from his sketches of the West at the National Academy of Design and the Centennial Exposition at Philadelphia in 1876. After the Indian Wars, Colyer focused on the Connecticut landscape for the remainder of his career. However, his watercolor and pencil sketches of the American West have

Fig. 10. Photograph of Frank Reaugh sketching in the field. Modern print from glass-plate negative, 5 x 7 in. (12.7 x 17.8 cm). Panhandle-Plains Historical Museum, Canyon, Texas, Frank Reaugh Estate.

become treasured documents of early southwestern art. Colyer's excursion took him near enough to sketch the Antelope Hills and Medicine Bluff, both sacred to Southern Plains tribes. In fact, his *On the Big Canadian River, May 1869* (fig. 8) may be the earliest known painting of the Texas Panhandle, and his paintings of western Indian Territory are almost certainly the earliest images after George Catlin's trip through Arkansas Territory in 1834.[16]

In the wake of the removal of Indians from West Texas and eastern New Mexico, Hispanic sheepherders, or *pastores*, from New Mexico Territory and Anglo cattlemen brought their respective herds into the Texas Panhandle. Charles Goodnight led the way for cattlemen in 1876, establishing the J A Ranch in lower Palo Duro with a herd from Colorado, followed closely by Thomas Sherman Bugbee with a herd from Kansas. In 1887, Goodnight invited Albert Bierstadt to paint in Palo Duro Canyon and on the J A Ranch.[17] Bierstadt declined but apparently suggested that Goodnight extend the invitation to John Clifford Cowles (1861–1951). Born in Illinois, Cowles may have studied at the National Academy of Design and the Art Students League in New York, and may also have worked in Paris. He painted the John Chisum Ranch in

Fig. 11. Frank Reaugh. **Sunrise on the Prairie.** *c. 1888. Pastel on paper, 5 5/8 x 8 3/4 in. (14.3 x 22.2 cm). Panhandle-Plains Historical Museum, Canyon, Texas, Frank Reaugh Estate.*

eastern New Mexico Territory in 1885, exhibited in Salt Lake City in 1894, and his large painting of Shoshone Falls hangs in the Idaho State House. The two works initially prompted by Bierstadt's recommendation, however, remain the earliest known oil paintings of Palo Duro Canyon. In *J A Panorama* (*Palo Duro Canyon*) (fig. 9), Cowles clearly shows Bierstadt's influence, even exaggerating the topography for dramatic effect as well as including fore- and middle-ground details similar to Bierstadt's *The Rocky Mountains, Lander's Peak.* By the 1870s, the Southwest had begun to appear on canvas.

The Visible Southwest:
Frank Reaugh, Transcendent Landscapes, and the Texas Plains

The painter who rose to the top of Southwestern art before 1900 is Charles Franklin "Frank" Reaugh (1860–1945). Born near Jacksonville, Illinois, in 1860, Reaugh first came to Texas with his family via wagon in 1876 at age fifteen. The Reaughs settled on a farm near Terrell until 1889 and then moved to Oak Cliff near Dallas. Reaugh had little formal education, but his mother, Clarinda Spillman Reaugh, was his teacher in all things. A Presbyterian minister's daughter, his mother instilled in her only child an appreciation of nature, grounded in books on zoology, botany, and natural history, and infused with the philosophies of famed Swiss scientist Louis Agassiz (1807–1873) and Transcendentalist John Burroughs. Clarinda Reaugh also encouraged her son's interest in the fine arts. Reaugh's father, George Washington Reaugh—mechanic, carpenter, cabinetmaker, farmer, and forty-niner—taught him to work with hand tools, and spurred his son's travels over the American West. As a way of developing his art, Reaugh studied cattle and sheep anatomy and sketched long-horn cattle brought up from South Texas. His reproductions of landscapes by Frederic Edwin Church as well as British painters John Constable, Horatio McCullough, Thomas Allom, and J. M. W. Turner appeared in popular magazines such as *Harper's*, *Scribner's*, and *Century Illustrated*.

In the early 1880s, Reaugh accompanied two cattlemen, brothers Frank and Jerome "Romeo" Houston, on cattle drives and roundups in northwest Texas and in Indian Territory. Probably with the Houstons, Reaugh made his first documented trip to "Western Texas" in 1883, likely near present-day Wichita Falls and Henrietta (fig. 10). Reaugh sketched from the saddle during these trips (fig. 11), and "referred to them the most" for his later cattle paintings.[18] He later enlarged and composed them as paintings in the studio. These field sketches resulted in his great early paintings, *Watering the Herd* (1889) (fig. 12), *February in Texas* (1893), *The O Roundup, Texas, 1888* (1894), and *The Approaching Herd* (1902).

Reaugh studied at the Saint Louis School of Fine Arts during the winter of 1884–85. In November 1888, he enrolled at the Académie Julian in Paris, a school popular with international students, especially Americans, because its admissions standards were less rigorous than those of the École des Beaux-Arts. However, professors of the École des Beaux-Arts taught and critiqued at the Académie Julian regularly, and Reaugh drew and painted from the figure there under the watchful eyes of Jules Lefebvre, John-Joseph Benjamin Constant, and Henri-Lucien Douciet, all members of the *juste milieu* in France. In addition to studying at the Académie Julian, Reaugh copied and studied paintings in the Louvre and the Luxembourg Palace.[19]

At the end of March 1889, Reaugh traveled through Belgium and the Netherlands, studying paintings of the Flemish and Dutch schools, and particularly those of The Hague School, popular in the United States at the time.[20] Reaugh returned to Paris in time to see the Exposition Universelle and, when his ship stopped in Liverpool, may have seen paintings by Turner. Reaugh returned to Texas at the end of May 1889.

Fig. 12. Frank Reaugh. **Watering the Herd.** *1889. Pastel on paper mounted on canvas, 18 1/8 x 34 3/8 in. (46 x 87.3 cm). Panhandle-Plains Historical Museum, Canyon, Texas, Frank Reaugh Estate.*

Between 1890 and 1915, Reaugh enjoyed his greatest critical success, exhibiting works at two world's fairs, the 1893 World's Columbian Exposition in Chicago and the 1904 Louisiana Purchase Exposition in St. Louis. He also exhibited at the National Academy of Design in New York, the Pennsylvania Academy of the Fine Arts in Philadelphia, the Carnegie Institute in Pittsburgh, and the Art Institute of Chicago. He had solo exhibitions with Chicago's Central Art Association in 1895 and in Colorado Springs in 1897. Moreover, Reaugh became a member of the Society of Western Artists and exhibited with that group throughout the United States. Finally, Reaugh toured his pastels with much success, especially in the upper Midwest. In Texas, Reaugh exhibited nearly annually at the State Fair of Texas until 1930 and at the Fort Worth Annual Texas Artists Exhibition from 1910 until 1937.[21]

Around 1890, Reaugh began using a camera as a sketching tool. While scholars have established that Reaugh never transferred a photographic image directly to a painting, he did use photographs in creating his landscapes. He made notes in the margins of his photographs referencing specific paintings.[22]

Outside the world of painting, Reaugh was a reader and disciple of John Burroughs, particularly appreciating the essayist's ability to locate God in nature. For Burroughs—as for the Transcendentalists and Romantics before him—there "comes a time when the mind perceives that this world is the work of God."

Fig. 13. Frank Reaugh. **Towards Head of Cañon.** *1893. Pastel on paper, 6 1/8 x 9 3/8 in. (15.6 x 23.8 cm). Panhandle-Plains Historical Museum, Canyon, Texas, Frank Reaugh Estate.*

Burroughs wrote, "In the order of nature we may behold the ways of the Eternal; in fact, . . . God is here and now in the humblest and most familiar fact, as sleepless and active as ever he was in old Judea."[23] Raised a Presbyterian yet rarely attending formal church services, Reaugh read scripture throughout his life and, in his art, found ways to express his love of Creator and creation. He sought to "worship [his] Creator" in "an environment conducive to a fitting frame of mind. . . . I often long for a church where I can worship alone and undisturbed; this being denied me I've taken to the woods. I guess I belong to nature's church which is about the only one this ultra-modern world has left unspoiled."[24]

Reaugh began his Southwestern sojourn in earnest in 1893, when he set out to paint the famed Palo Duro Canyon. Armed with letters of introduction to Charles Goodnight and the manager of the J A Ranch, Reaugh painted and photographed Goodnight's buffalo pasture and made several pastels of the canyon (fig. 13). On this trip, Reaugh was probably the first artist to paint and photograph the hoodoo—a natural column of rock—in the canyon that today is called the "Lighthouse" and is a defining landmark for Palo Duro Canyon. Reaugh called this feature "The Grand Chimney," producing several versions in pastel and oil. He probably painted Palo Duro Canyon more than any artist, exhibiting his Palo Duro paintings in Chicago as early as 1895. *The Chicago Record* called Reaugh's *Palo Duro Canyon #7* "dramatic. . . .

Fig. 14. Albert Bierstadt. **Indians Spear Fishing.** *1862. Oil on canvas, 19 1/4 x 29 1/4 in. (48.9 x 74.3 cm). The Museum of Fine Arts, Houston, gift of the family of Joseph S. Cullinan, and Mr. and Mrs. David R. Wintermann, by exchange, with additional gifts from Mr. and Mrs. Harry C. Wiess; Mrs. E. L. Perry; Mr. and Mrs. John H. Blaffer in memory of his father, Robert Lee Blaffer; Edith A. and Percy S. Straus; Grand Central Art Galleries; Miss Ima Hogg; General and Mrs. Maurice Hirsch; the Allied Arts Association; Mr. and Mrs. Charles L. Bybee; Nan Greacen Faure; Helen M. Turner; Mr. and Mrs. Herbert Levine; the Axson Club, Houston; William Best; Sarah Campbell Blaffer; Mrs. Willimina Borland; Mrs. Evan W. Burris; the Houston Art League through the bequest of George M. Dickson; Miss Katherine S. Dreier; George Wharton Edwards; Parker Edwards; Mrs. William Stamps Farish; the Houston Friends of Art; Angela MacDonnell; Mrs. Justine Franklin McGuire; the Smithsonian Institution; Harmand Teplow; the University Club of Houston; Robert C. Vose, in memory of Seth M. Vose; Nelson Waggener; Emile Walters; and Irene Weir, all by exchange (2008.226).*

The landscape, moreover, is peculiarly sympathetic making the ensemble a thing of high excellence in point of conception."[25] Reaugh returned periodically to Palo Duro and the nearby Tule Canyon until the 1930s, often bringing his students to paint in the canyonlands in a converted Model-T dubbed the Cicada.

Reaugh's paintings and travels were not limited to northwest Texas, however. His journeys ranged from the northwestern-most corner of the Panhandle south to the Big Bend of the Rio Grande and west to the Arizona–New Mexico border. Setting out on trips that took him up the various forks and breaks of the Brazos, Wichita, Red, Canadian, Concho, Pease, and Pecos rivers, and to mountains with lyrical names such as Guadalupe, Christmas, and Organ, he painted nearly everything he encountered. First on horseback, then in a Studebaker hack, Reaugh traveled throughout the Southwest. Besides Palo Duro in the Panhandle, Reaugh also painted in the far western part of Texas; he traveled to El Paso in 1892, and the Davis and Chisos mountains became favorite haunts. Cathedral Mountain, in the Davis Mountains between Alpine and Marathon in northwestern Brewster County, Texas, became a frequent subject. As Reaugh painted tributes to the Southwest in his canvases, he echoed those same rhapsodies of nature expressed by John Burroughs and John Muir. For these wanderers in a new wilderness, worship happened out of doors, where the divine presence dwelled and became accessible to the wanderer and reverent seer. Muir, in his beloved Yosemite, found in Cathedral Peak a "temple displaying Nature's best masonry and sermons in stones. . . . This I may say is the first time I have been at church in California, led here at last, every door graciously opened for the poor lonely worshiper. In our best times everything turns into religion, all the world seems a church and the mountains altars."[26]

The Plains also fascinated Reaugh. In his pastel, *The O Roundup, Texas, 1888*, he echoes William Cullen Bryant's 1832 epic *The Prairies*:

These are the gardens of the Desert, these
The unshorn fields, boundless and beautiful,
For which the speech of England has no name—
The Prairies . . .

.　　　.　　　.　　　.　　　.　　　.　　　.

The sunny ridges. Breezes of the South!
Who toss the golden and the flame-like flowers,
And pass the prairie-hawk that, poised on high,
Flaps his broad wings, yet moves not—ye have played
Among the palms of Mexico and vines
Of Texas . . .

.　　　.　　　.　　　.　　　.　　　.　　　.

A nobler or a lovelier scene than this?
Man hath no power in all this glorious work:
The hand that built the firmament hath heaved
And smoothed these verdant swells, and sown their slopes
With herbage, planted them with island groves,
And hedged them round with forests. Fitting floor
For this magnificent temple of the sky.[27]

*Fig. 15. Louis Oscar Griffith. **Cows in the Milkweed***. *c. 1906. Oil on canvasboard, 9 7/8 x 12 1/8 in. (25.1 x 30.8 cm). Panhandle-Plains Historical Museum, Canyon, Texas, Friends of Southwestern Art Purchase.*

The (Chicago) Sunday Inter Ocean echoed Bryant in its review of the painting: "'The Roundup' is undoubtedly the picture of the Reaugh collections. The picture is soft and beautiful in coloring, slightly luminous, with pearly qualities in the landscape. There is no vivid color. But there is distance and a wonderful sky. It is really a beautiful picture and a good one."[28] Painted from sketches made northwest of Fort Belknap in 1888, the roundup depicted was the largest Reaugh had seen, with fifteen thousand head of cattle, a hundred cowboys, and six to seven hundred horses.

In addition to West Texas, Reaugh painted all over the Southwest, in the Northern Plains, and even in California. He painted the geysers on the Firehole River in Yellowstone, and he considered his *Powder River* his finest landscape in oil. While working in Conejos Canyon in Colorado in 1897, he painted his famous *Pike's Peak from Garden of the Gods* and several other works. His Colorado work was exhibited at Colorado Springs in 1897. Reaugh also worked frequently in Arizona, taking a sketching group there as late as 1920. His pastels of the Grand Canyon and his several paintings of San Francisco Peak recall works by the Hudson River School painters Church, Bierstadt, and Moran. Indeed, Reaugh maintained

Fig. 16. Edward G. Eisenlohr. **Untitled (Dusty Road).** *c. 1900. Oil on canvas, 24 x 34 7/8 in. (61 x 88.6 cm). Panhandle-Plains Historical Museum, Canyon, Texas, gift of Gertrude Helmle.*

his allegiance to the Hudson River School methodology, as seen in his *Watering the Herd* (see fig. 12), or by comparing the atmospheric affect in Reaugh's view of the Chisos Mountains wrapped in a storm to Bierstadt's *Indians Spear Fishing* (fig. 14). Here again is the Sublime landscape, filled with the power of God personified in the mildly terrifying storm in the mountains—visual reminders of a power greater than ourselves.

Times of Transition

Reaugh began taking students to the Southwest as early as 1890, when Charles Peter Bock and L. O. Griffith accompanied him on trips to the Wichita River. Bock (b. 1872) of Manvel, Texas, studied at the Art Institute and Art Students League of Chicago and accompanied Reaugh again to the Llano Estacado in 1908. Traveling with Reaugh to Wichita in 1905 was Indiana-born and Dallas-raised Louis Oscar Griffith (1875–1956) (fig. 15). As a child, Griffith studied with Reaugh in Dallas, and later studied at the Saint Louis School of Fine Arts, the Art Institute of Chicago, and the National Academy of Design, becoming an established printmaker.

Above: Fig. 17. S. Seymour Thomas. **Untitled (Stock Tank)**. c. 1898. Oil on canvas, 14 x 20 in. (36.6 x 50.8 cm). Panhandle-Plains Historical Museum, Canyon, Texas, purchase funded by Cynthia and Bill Gayden.

Left: Fig. 18. William Robinson Leigh. **In the Granville Gorge, Tower of Isis—Colorado River**. 1910. Oil on canvas, 33 x 27 in. (83.8 x 68.6 cm). Panhandle-Plains Historical Museum, Canyon, Texas, Johnie Griffin Collection.

In 1911, Edward G. Eisenlohr (1872–1961) was part of Reaugh's "Trans-Llano Sketching Association," and his experience was recorded in a small booklet whose photographs and maps reveals much about the primitive nature of these Reaugh sketching trips.[29] Born in Cincinnati, Eisenlohr settled in Dallas and studied with Texas masters Reaugh and Robert Onderdonk, at the Art Students League summer school at Woodstock, New York, and at the Karlsruhe Academy at Karlsruhe, Germany. His work was exhibited at the Corcoran Gallery, Washington, D.C., the National Academy of Design, and the Museum of Modern Art, New York, and at the Texas Centennial Exposition. An annual summer resident of Santa Fe, Eisenlohr contributed significantly to Southwestern art, and his *Untitled* (*Dusty Road*) (fig. 16) is exemplary of his early work.

Although he did not study under Reaugh, S. Seymour Thomas (1868–1956) painted landscapes around San Antonio and contributed to the growth of Southwest painting (fig. 17). He became an expatriate, living in Paris from 1888 until 1913, but occasionally returned to Texas. Born in San Augustine in East Texas, Thomas lived in Dallas and San Antonio before studying at the Art Students League in New York, and the Académie Julian in Paris. Thomas moved back to the United States, living first in New York, then in California. He exhibited at the Paris Salons and several world's fairs and was commissioned to do a monumental portrait of Sam Houston for the World's Columbian Exposition at Chicago in 1893.

Part of the late-nineteenth-century expansion of culture and art into the Southwest, the all-important railroads brought in tourists and dollars, hiring artists to promote their lines. The Atchison, Topeka, and Santa Fe Railway eventually amassed a collection of nearly four hundred paintings, housed at its corporate headquarters in Chicago. Among the artists included was William Robinson Leigh (1866–1955), who trained at the Royal Academy in Munich from 1883 to 1896 and contributed illustrations to *Scribner's Magazine* upon his return to the United States. He traveled to the West beginning in 1906, and his *In the Granville Gorge, Tower of Isis—Colorado River* (fig. 18) resulted from sketches made on a 1908 Santa Fe Railroad-sponsored trip to the Grand Canyon.

During this period of transition around the turn of the century, artists were seeking new venues, away from the dirt and pollution of cities. As artists established art colonies from Provincetown to Santa Barbara, they also found their way to the American Southwest. Simultaneously, European Modernism gained influence in the American art vernacular, and painting began to move away from transcendental

*Fig. 19. Bert Geer Phillips. **Untitled (Indian Portrait).** c. 1907. Oil on academy board, 10 1/8 x 8 1/8 in. (25.7 x 20.6 cm). Panhandle-Plains Historical Museum, Canyon, Texas, gift of Mary and William Klingensmith in memory of Lucile Klingensmith and Gertrude Wetzel.*

and even spiritual subjects. The influence of the Hudson River School was receding. Nevertheless, the old ways died hard, and the last remnants of Transcendentalism, the seeing of God in nature, still lingered—albeit only as a breath.

The founding of the well-known Taos art colony is part of this transition in early twentieth-century American art. In 1898, Bert Geer Phillips (1868–1956) became the first resident artist in Taos and created an art colony there (fig. 19). Writing to his painting partner, Ernest L. Blumenschein (1874–1960), Phillips extolled the opportunities for painters in Santa Fe: "For heaven's sake, tell people what we have found! Send some artists out here. There is a lifetime's work for twenty men." Blumenschein responded and first viewed the Taos Valley and the Sangre de Cristo range in 1898:

Fig. 20. Gerald Cassidy. **Master of Ceremonies.** *1925. Oil on canvas, 18 x 18 1/8 in. (45.7 x 46 cm). Panhandle-Plains Historical Museum, Canyon, Texas, Johnie Griffin Collection.*

Fig. 21. Sheldon Parsons. **Santa Fe Fall.** *c. 1913. Oil on board, 20 x 16 in. (50.8 x 40.6 cm). Panhandle-Plains Historical Museum, Canyon, Texas, by exchange.*

Stretching away from the foot of the range was a vast plateau cut by the Rio Grande and by lesser gorges in which were located small villages of flat-roofed adobe houses built around a church and plaza, all fitting into the color scheme of the tawny surroundings. The Sky was a clear, clean blue with sharp moving clouds. The color, the effective character of the landscape, the drama of the vast spaces, the superb beauty and serenity of the hills, stirred me deeply. I realized I was getting my own uniqueness from nature, seeing it for the first time with my own eyes, uninfluenced by the art of any man.[30]

After his initial trip to Taos, Blumenschein would not return until 1910. The colony, however, grew, and on the heels of Blumenschein's first visit and Phillips's arrival came others—Oscar Berninghaus in 1899, E. Irving Couse in 1902, Joseph H. Sharp's first visit in 1893 and his return in 1908, and W. Herbert Dunton in 1912.

These six artists founded the Taos Society of Artists in July 1915 and would influence Southwestern art for decades to come.

Meanwhile, some seventy miles south in Santa Fe, a much less concerted effort to create an art colony began in 1904 with the arrival of Carlos Vierra (1876–1937), the city's first resident artist. Warren E. Rollins (1861–1962), who had visited New Mexico in 1893, returned to teach classes at the Palace of the Governors by 1910. Gerald Cassidy (1879–1934) had moved to Albuquerque by 1890, then to Santa Fe in 1912 (fig. 20). And Sheldon Parsons (1866–1943) had come to Santa Fe for health reasons in 1913 (fig. 21). These "old guard" Santa Fe artists paralleled their *compadres* in Taos to the north, both stylistically and philosophically. Even so, the artists of the early New Mexico colonies, while not opposed to seeing the hand of God in the Southwest, were not necessarily carrying on the traditions influenced by the Transcendentalists and the Hudson River School of locating and illuminating the work of the divine in American nature.

It remained for Frank Reaugh to carry this torch, displayed on canvases in the Catskill Mountains of New York as it had been in the inkwells of Emerson and his fellows. In fact, it is fitting to compare Eisenlohr's portrait of Reaugh, standing in an arid Southwestern landscape, in his *My Country 'Tis of Thee* with Emerson's famous sketch of himself as a "transparent eyeball" in *Nature*. There, on New England ground, a new American seer left behind individual limitations, "became nothing," and blended upward and outward with the air and "infinite space." God's vistas "uplift[ed]" him and, merging with an unending distance, Emerson felt "part and particle of God." In 1836, Divine Nature was the Sublime and Beautiful setting into which Emerson merged, and it became the land that Reaugh would illuminate in his own tributes to the open skies and brilliant colors of the American Southwest:

> I like to be where the skies are unstained by dust and smoke, where the trees are untrimmed and where the wild flowers grow. I like the brilliant sunlight, and the far distance. I like the opalescent color of the plains. It is the beauty of the great Southwest as God has made it that I love to paint.[31]

Notes

1 Ralph Waldo Emerson, *Nature* (1836).

2 John Burroughs, *Accepting the Universe* (Boston and New York: Houghton Mifflin, 1920; repr. in *Universal Pantheist Society Newsletter,* summer 1978, Universal Pantheist Society), http://www.pantheist.net/society/god_of_pantheism.html.

3 Edmund Burke, *Philosophical Inquiry into the Origin of Our Ideas of the Sublime and Beautiful* (1757; repr., eBooks@Adelaide, University of Adelaide Library, Australia, 2007), http://ebooks.adelaide.edu.au/b/burke/edmund/sublime/.

4 William Wordsworth, "Lines Written a Few Miles above Tintern Abbey, On Revisiting the Banks of the Wye During a Tour" (1798; repr. RCHS Hypertext Reader), http://www.rc.umd.edu/rchs/reader/tabbey.html, lines 97–103.

5 For the best discussion of Cole in this context, see Barbara Novak, *American Painting of the Nineteenth Century: Realism, Idealism, and the American Experience,* 2nd edition (New York: Harper and Row, 1979), 61–79.

6 James Thomas Flexner, *That Wilder Image: The Paintings of America's Native School from Thomas Cole to Winslow Homer* (New York: Bonanza Books, 1962), 45.

7 On Durand, see Novak, *American Painting,* 80–91.

8 Joseph Henry and Spencer Fullerton Baird, United States Army, United States War Dept., *Reports of explorations and surveys, to ascertain the most practicable and economical route for a railroad from the Mississippi River to the Pacific Ocean,* vol. 3 (Washington, D.C.: Government Printing Office, 1856).

9 John Muir to Catharine Merrill, Yosemite (1872), in *John Muir: His Life and Letters and Other Writings* (Seattle: The Mountaineers, 1996), 167.

10 Bierstadt to John Hay, 22 August 1863, John Hay Collection, John Hay Library, Brown University, Providence, R.I., quoted in Nancy Anderson and Linda Ferber, *Albert Bierstadt: Art and Enterprise* (New York: Hudson Hills Press in association with the Brooklyn Museum, 1990), 178.

11 John Muir, *My First Summer in the Sierra* (Boston and New York: Houghton Mifflin, 1911), 211.

12 For a fascinating study on this trip, see Nancy Dustin Wall Moure, "Five Eastern Artists Out West," *American Art Journal* 5 (November 1973): 15–31.

13 Ralph Waldo Emerson, "The Poet," in *Essays: Second Series* (Boston: James Munroe, 1844), 211.

14 For additional discussion of these traditions in Texas, see Sam Ratcliffe's essay in this volume.

15 Congress created the Board of Indian Commissioners in April 1869 as part of President Grant's "peace policy." Later, Colyer traveled to the Pacific Northwest and Alaska on a similar assignment.

16 Due to illness, Catlin never crossed the Red River into Texas.

17 See Charles Goodnight letterpress book, Research Center, Panhandle-Plains Historical Museum, Canyon, Texas.

18 See Frank Reaugh, *Paintings of the Southwest* (Dallas: Wilkinson Printing Company, 1937), 12.

19 "[John] Russell, of England, and [Maurice Quentin de] La Tour, [Jean-Etienne] Liotard, [Jean-Siméon] Chardin, and [Élisabeth Vigée] Le Brun. These were great painters. . . . the work of all of them may be seen in the pastel room of the Louvre, as fresh and bright, apparently, as on the day [they were] done." In addition to the pastellists he mentioned, Reaugh also saw pastels in the Louvre by Rosalba Carriera, François Boucher, and Pierre-Paul Prud'hon. Frank Reaugh, *Pastel* (Dallas: Reaugh Studios, 1927), n.p.

20 Many writers have reported that Reaugh studied with Anton Mauve. This is a serious error, as Mauve was dead by 1888. More correctly, Reaugh studied the paintings of Mauve.

21 Reaugh's work was featured at the Fort Worth Frontier Centennial Exposition and the Golden Jubilee Exposition at the State Fair of Texas in 1939.

22 I have only seen one Reaugh painting based directly on a Reaugh photograph, *Grazing the Herd*; otherwise, it seems he used his photographs more as reminders than images to copy.

23 John Burroughs, *The Light of Day: Religious Discussions and Criticisms from the Naturalist's Point of View* (Boston and New York: Houghton Mifflin, 1900), 50–51.

24 Frank Reaugh, *Biographical* (Dallas, 1936), n.p.

25 *The Chicago Record*, 14 March 1895.

26 Muir, *My First Summer in the Sierra*, 336.

27 William Cullen Bryant, "The Prairies" (1832, repr. in "William Cullen Bryant" website, ed. Ann Woodlief, 2010), http://www.vcu.edu/engweb/webtexts/Bryant/prairies.html.

28 *The (Chicago) Sunday Inter Ocean*, 10 March 1895.

29 This booklet is housed in the Frank Reaugh Collection, Research Center, Panhandle-Plains Historical Museum, Canyon, Texas.

30 Ernest L. Blumenschein, quoted in Laura Bickerstaff, *Pioneer Artists of Taos* (Denver: Sage Books, 1955), 30–31.

31 Reaugh, *Biographical*, n.p.

Contributors

Russell Versaci is Principal of Russell Versaci Architecture, Middleburg, Virginia.

Sam Ratcliffe is Head of the Bywaters Special Collections, Hamon Arts Library, Southern Methodist University, Dallas, Texas.

Kenneth Hafertepe is Chair and Director of Graduate Studies, Department of Museum Studies, Baylor University, Waco, Texas.

Maurie D. McInnis is Associate Professor and Associate Dean for Undergraduate Academic Programs, the University of Virginia, Charlottesville, Virginia.

Michael R. Grauer is Associate Director for Curatorial Affairs and Curator of Art, Panhandle-Plains Historical Museum, Canyon, Texas.

Photograph Credits

Front cover and frontispiece: Photographs by Thomas R. DuBrock, department of photographic and imaging services, the Museum of Fine Arts, Houston.
Back cover and page xiii: Photographs by Rick Gardner.

Roots of Home: An Architectural Tourist in the South
Russell Versaci
Figs. 1–4, 9, 10, 14, 15, 19, 23, 24, 27, 29: Historic American Buildings Survey.
Fig. 5: Russell Versaci Architecture.
Figs. 6, 7, 11, 13, 14, 20, 21, 25, 26, 30: Photographs by Erik Kvalsvik.
Fig. 8: Photograph courtesy Cumming Map Society.
Fig. 28: Photograph by Ignacio Salas-Humara.

Romanticism Goes West: Nineteenth-Century European Painters in Texas
Sam Ratcliffe
Figs. 3, 4, 5, 6, 26, 34: Photographs by Thomas R. DuBrock, department of photographic and imaging services, the Museum of Fine Arts, Houston.

Fachwerk, Log, and Rock: German Texans' Houses
Kenneth Hafertepe
Fig. 13: Courtesy Volz and Associates.
Fig. 25: Texas Parks and Wildlife.

Scarlett Doesn't Live Here Anymore: Tara, Gone with the Wind, and the Southern Landscape Tradition
Maurie McInnis
Fig. 1: © 1939 M-G-M/Turner Entertainment Co. All rights reserved. Photograph: Photofest.
Fig. 5: © Image Gibbes Museum of Art/Carolina Art Association.
Fig. 11: ® Sears Brands, LLC.

As God Has Made It: Painting the American Southwest before 1900
Michael R. Grauer
Figs. 2, 3, 4, 5, 14: Photographs by Thomas R. DuBrock, department of photographic and imaging services, the Museum of Fine Arts, Houston.